THE VOICE OF
LIBERAL LEARNING

THE VOICE OF LIBERAL LEARNING

Michael Oakeshott on Education

Edited by Timothy Fuller

YALE UNIVERSITY PRESS
NEW HAVEN AND LONDON 1989

Library of Congress Cataloging-in-Publication Data

Oakeshott, Michael Joseph, 1901–
  The voice of liberal learning.

  Includes bibliographical references and index.
  1. Education—Philosophy—1965–   . 2. Education,
Higher—1965–   . I. Fuller, Timothy, 1940–
I. Title
LB41.0177   1989   378'.001   88-27811
ISBN 0-300-04344-9 (cloth)
ISBN 0-300-04753-3 (paper)

Set in Linotron Baskerville by Best-set
Typesetter, Hong Kong

Printed in Great Britain at
The Bath Press, Avon

CONTENTS

INTRODUCTION

Timothy Fuller

A Philosophical Understanding of Education

Those who know Michael Oakeshott will insist that first and foremost he is a great teacher. He, on the other hand, has always thought of himself, first, as a learner. His schooldays, he will tell you, were the happiest time of his life. And it was his never forgotten experience as a schoolboy that led him to become a teacher and the kind of teacher he was: unavoidably a lecturer and a critic of his pupils' work, but more at home in the conversational give-and-take of a class or a seminar; a guide rather than an instructor, a fellow-traveller rather than a leader.

Being philosophically disposed to consider what he was doing as well as doing it, it is not surprising that he should often have reflected on the engagements of teaching and learning and from time to time have published these reflections. For the most part, what he has written on these subjects was composed for specific occasions, was published locally, and is now out of print. The present purpose is to reprint the more significant of these pieces in the belief that what was prompted by particular occasions has more than local value for those who are committed to liberal learning.

How teaching and learning are characterized in these essays springs from, and presupposes, the philosophical understanding of human experience which Oakeshott explored in his first major work, *Experience and its Modes* (1933), and which was elaborated in the first part of *On Human Conduct* (1975).

The quest to identify the distinctive features of important human

I

activities has always been central to his philosophical investigations. He is most widely known for expounding the central features
of the political life, for elaborating his ideal of civil association, for
his work on the nature of the historian's activity and on the idea of
the rule of law. The essays collected here should reveal that seeking
the distinguishing features of teaching and learning are inseparable
from his work as a whole.[1]

Oakeshott's essays evoke the elusive features inherent in good
teaching and learning without obscuring the great variability in
manners of teaching which defy generalization. Contemporary
efforts to simplify teaching into a set of technical functions, so
that it might become 'fail-safe', is a disastrous misunderstanding,
however well-intentioned, threatening to destroy the possibility of
genuine learning.

Both in Britain and the United States there are great debates
about the future of education at every level. It is widely accepted
that there are fundamental derangements within the educational
establishments, and proposals for reform or revolution abound.
Opinions range from denying that there is any particular thing
that should be learned to asserting that there is a canonical short-
list of great books to which teachers and students should confine
themselves exclusively. Educational experts try their hand at
drawing up check-lists of general information which purport to
describe 'what every student should know'. Programmes for making education socially relevant abound. Arguments rage over the
place of Western civilization in the curriculum as if a civilization
were an offering we could choose simply to accept or reject, an
object of detached investigation.

Liberal learning as Oakeshott understands it has been confused
with, or displaced by, 'behaviour modification' in the minds of
many: sex education, drug education, values clarification, peace
studies, suicide prevention ('death education'), consciousness rais-
ing, and much else that enjoys current celebrity.

In such a pot-pourri there is no clear judgement of the distinguishing features of teaching and learning, nor of the character of

[1] Oakeshott is well known in intellectual and academic circles for his remarkable introduction to Hobbes's *Leviathan* (1946), for *Experience and its Modes* (1933), *Rationalism in
Politics* (1962), *On Human Conduct* (1975), and *On History* (1983). However, with the excep-
tion of two essays included in *Rationalism in Politics*, 'Political Education' and 'The Study of
Politics in a University', his reflections on education have not as yet gained wide circula-
tion. For more complete bibliographical information, the reader should consult *Politics and
Experience, Essays Presented to Michael Oakeshott*, edited by Preston King and B. C. Parekh
(Cambridge: Cambridge University Press, 1968), and Josiah Lee Auspitz, 'Bibliographical
Note', *Political Theory*, vol. 4, no. 3, August 1976, pp. 295–300.

the places where those activities have traditionally been undertaken. Proposals for curriculum reform often take no account of the existing practices into which they must be fitted. We are in peril of forgetting that it was the perception of their special qualities that inspired the setting apart of places of learning, and justified their special privileges of leisure and free discussion, in Europe and North America over the past eight centuries.

It is often alleged that there is no longer any basis of agreement, apart perhaps from features of technique, to aid reflection on what teaching and learning are about. Academicians alternatively feel liberated or coerced to pick and choose among the vast array of alternatives before them. More and more options arise not from the mutual self-exploration of those who are intimately and continually engaged in the academic enterprise – teachers and scholars – but from those who wish to mine the academy's 'mental resources', whether to perfect or to undermine current social policies, and who give or withhold support of the academy for these reasons. Under such conditions, it ought not to surprise anyone that educational institutions, both in Great Britain and the United States, have become less distinguishable from pressure groups seeking protection for their interests.

Academic institutions nowadays are often little more than weak alliances among intellectual entrepreneurs who welcome the intervention of extrinsic goals and 'values', and the money that supports them from foundation and government grants. This must alter the conversation among academics. Frequently, they cooperate entirely with a view to mutual protection, through studied indifference, of their separate intellectual interests. This is not the agreement to disagree, which has always been essential to academic life; it is an agreement to be ignorant of each other, and to avoid reflections that might carry them beyond the plying of their respective disciplinary trades.

Academic institutions, it would appear, are in varying degrees disintegrated communities of scholars. They remain places physically set apart for teaching and learning, but entering their premises no longer guarantees encounter with a self-understanding, however mysterious and complex it may initially seem, that gradually discloses a distinctive manner of activity that really does set them apart. What has been obscured, if not lost, is the *idea* of a school, a college, a university.

It is important to emphasize the danger this loss entails. Many mistakenly assume that what is missing is an organizing, energizing purpose or goal for education. It is characteristic of our time to look for ulterior purposes, and to design programmes to achieve them, rather than to recall what we have already learned how to do and to take that as our guide. Since the world is overflowing with purposes and programmes, it is an increasingly irresistible temptation for academic institutions to submit to the world's inevitably contradictory judgements.

Yet, for Michael Oakeshott, the idea of an activity is necessarily, inevitably, interwoven with, and emergent from within, the continuous practice of the activity. If we do not now find it easy to pick out the salient features of teaching and learning, it is in part because we do not now enjoy a clarifying experience of them.

We are sorely tempted to focus our attention on techniques rather than on the qualities that inhere in those whose mastery of a subject is such that, without doting on abstract techniques, perhaps without ever having even tried to conceptualize techniques apart from the practice of an activity, they appear before us as masters whose conduct we may imitate as apprentices, absorbing the idea and the practice in a harmonious whole.

Oakeshott's reflections on teaching and learning uniquely attend to just these neglected features. He offers no check-list of things that every educated person ought to know. The check-list approach must narrow the sense of adventure into uncharted intellectual seas, obscuring the point that one is educated not merely because of what one knows, but as much or more for the manner in which one learns.

In saying the latter, one runs the risk of confusing emphasis on the manner of learning with Deweyite emphasis on skills and the accompanying de-emphasis on the content of learning. But for Oakeshott the aim is to enter a relationship of 'conversation' informed by familiarity with the traditional literary, philosophical, artistic and scientific expressions of European civilization. There is no plausible distinction for him between 'essence' and 'accident', and thus no true learning that separates the 'how' from the 'what' of knowing. To try, therefore, to correct the last several generations of training in abstract skills, by creating a great debate over lists of books to be inserted in curricula, is to perpetuate an uncivilizing dichotomy (already evident in faculty debates), a bifurcating conflict unmediated by intimacy with a comprehensive tradition within which one can live and move, holding skill and knowledge together in a natural, experiential unity.

E. D. Hirsch in *Cultural Literacy* exemplifies this difficulty in continuing to defend the Deweyite aspirations to universal, democratic literacy while rejecting exclusive emphasis on skills he traces to Dewey and Rousseau.[2] He finds himself compelled to employ the great books as resources for creating 'cultural literacy', a facility in recognizing the use of literary allusions in contemporary writing that falls between mere functional literacy and expert knowledge of any subject. Such facility, Hirsch argues, will promote success in making one's way through life, and can also serve to create a common body of discourse among the diverse groups that modern polities must comprise. Laudable as the emphasis on rediscovering the great books and their memorable expressions may be, Hirsch has liberated himself very little from the technique orientation.[3]

Contemporary education is hard-pressed to distinguish formality and civility – the general rules of 'conversation' – from manipulative, managerial techniques which are designed to achieve goals of apparent specificity such as 'cultural literacy'. The project is to harness technique to an array of cultural artefacts, justified by reference to a certain conception of social improvement. Here we see the premises upon which much of the contemporary advocacy of 'general education' rests. Hirsch undoubtedly hopes students will discover, in the process, the experience of learning as an end in itself, but his justification is couched in terms of practical success. This approach lends itself particularly well to rhetorically powerful formulations by governmental agencies, promoting the prospect of solving educational 'problems' by 'educational policies'.

For Oakeshott, the conversation of liberal learning is mistakenly characterized when set in terms of 'progress' or of political programmes and policies. Nor does he think that real conversation can be 'general'. He speaks out of an experience of teaching and learning which is specific and yet broad in scope; this is not 'general'. 'General' education is a notion developed in response to 'specialized' or vocational education, and often implicitly understood to mean an adornment to practical training. The defectiveness of the term lies in the fact that it is spawned in reaction to the dominant tendencies of a culture prone to express itself in terms of 'prag-

---

[2] E. D. Hirsch, Jr., *Cultural Literacy: What Every American Needs to Know* (Boston: Houghton-Mifflin, 1987).

[3] Speaking of the need for cultural literacy in a modern, technological society, Hirsch writes: 'The complex undertakings of modern life depend on the co-operation of many people with different specialties in different places. Where communications fail, so do the undertakings. (That is the moral of the story of the Tower of Babel.)' *Cultural Literacy*, p. 2. Hirsch converts the Tower of Babel story into a parable for creating global unity through a joint technological enterprise requiring a universal form of literacy (communications skill). One might have taken the story to be a warning against such pretensions. Cultural literacy here means facility in employing a story from the past for a present purpose at odds with the original moral point. This perhaps illustrates something about 'cultural literacy' that should concern us.

matism', 'utility', 'technology', 'social design' and 'public policy'. It is now common, for example, in American colleges and universities, to speak of 'non-science majors' when referring to students of the humanities. Nowhere will one hear of science students as 'non-humanities majors'. This colloquialism is symptomatic of a cultural barrier to liberal learning, which is neither 'general' nor 'specialized' in the sense of 'vocational' or 'professional'.

In the essays that follow, Oakeshott evokes the idea of liberal learning, offering a corrective to those who, finding it difficult to set out quickly what education is about, wish to assuage their fears about its relevance.

If philosophical reflection on education is reduced to arguments solely about which books or concepts must be taught, we will remain in the impasse between confusion and dogma. It is characteristic nowadays to be so caught, in education, in politics, and in every important activity.

Oakeshott, seeking to circumvent these impasses whenever he encounters them, portrays an alternative vision which might help us to pass between anarchy on one side and the imposition of false doctrines of salvation on the other. That is why the metaphor of conversation is so central to his ideas of philosophy and of education. To see this, we must examine the general contours of his thought in relation to his educational reflections.

2

In *Experience and its Modes*, Oakeshott argued for the radical unity of human experience in thought.[4] He criticized as misleading all lingering dualistic distinctions such as immanent–transcendent, temporal–eternal, mediate–immediate experience; all efforts to postulate experience that is not within thought.[5] Our world, he asserted, is what we understand it to be; a 'world' emanates from human reflection and is thus a world of ideas. We are born and grow up in a world of ideas already present and understood in various ways by those preceding us on the scene, and we must learn its

---

[4] *Experience and its Modes* (Cambridge: Cambridge University Press, 1933). For example: 'experience is a single whole, within which modifications may be distinguished, but which admits of no final or absolute division; and that experience everywhere, not merely is inseparable from thought, but is itself a form of thought.' p. 10.

[5] 'It is, indeed, nonsensical to speak of reality as if it belonged to a separate world of its own. Either it is a character of the world of experience, or it must confess itself a nonentity. It is not a unique substance, but a predicative conception appropriate only to a world of experience. And the thinker who demands a reality beyond experience is certain of disappointment.' *Experience and its Modes*, p. 54.

features, interpret them and appropriate them to ourselves. Human beings are what they learn to become within an already ongoing world of ideas which they discover in their unsought entrance into it. From the outset, each of us encounters a world presented to us by others as something already understood, compelling us to seek to understand what others seem already to understand.

The relation between oneself and others is one of tension in search of reconciliation, incoherency in quest of coherency. We are neither free, in so far as we cannot choose some other world to escape to, nor are we determined, because our reconciliation to the already existing world depends on our own efforts to interpret it. Freedom means the interpretative response of human intelligence to encountered circumstances, most of which we have had little hand in creating.

Freedom, in this sense, is an inherent feature of human existence, which begins to show itself from the moment human beings make their appearance. Freedom is not a condition to be won, but a presupposition of conscious existence.[6] As such, freedom can appear to be either a blessing or a curse depending on individual responses, and human beings will affirm or deny the desirability of this freedom accordingly. 'Victory does not demonstrate this freedom nor defeat qualify it.'[7] But all human action, *qua* human action, presupposes intelligence at work. Freedom, intelligence, and interpretative response are woven together. Where intelligence is at work, freedom must be present.[8]

At any given moment, reflection tends to divide the totality of

---

[6] 'The starting-place of doing is a state of reflective consciousness, namely, the agent's own understanding of his situation, what it means to him. And, of course, it is no less *his* situation even though it may be a concern with what he understands to be the situation of another or of others. In this understanding, the situation is identified in specific terms; it is never the recognition of it as, for example, merely pleasurable or painful, rightful or wrongful. And it is in respect of this starting-place in an understood contingent situation that the agent in conduct may be said to be "free".' *On Human Conduct* (Oxford: Clarendon Press, 1975), p. 37.

[7] *On Human Conduct*, p. 40.

[8] 'The self-understanding of the agent...may be small, his powers of self-determination may be modest, he may be easily imposed upon, he may be duped into acting, but he is what he understands himself to be, his contingent situations are what he understands them to be, and the actions and utterances in which he responds to them are self-disclosures and self-enactments. He has a "history", but no "nature"; he is what in conduct he becomes. This "history" is not an evolutionary or teleological process. It is what he enacts for himself in a diurnal engagement, the unceasing articulation of understood responses to endlessly emergent understood situations which continues until he quits the diurnal scene. And although he may imagine an "ideal" human character and may use this character to direct his self-enactments, there is no ultimate or perfect man hidden in the womb of time or prefigured in the characters who now walk the earth.' *On Human Conduct*, p. 41.

experience into various modes through which that totality is interpreted. A mode of experience is an emergent line of thought or
practice within experience as a whole, a line which attempts to get
a grip on the whole, to make experience wholly coherent or man-
ageable from its own point of view. It is an inference from, and
potentially an assertion about, what the whole of experience must
be like in the absence of seeing the whole as such. Yet being abstract, all modes necessarily misrepresent the whole.[9] Most people
most of the time are content to understand the world within the
orderly framework of a particular mode's construction of the world,
or they patch together a perspective out of elements gleaned from
the more disciplined bodies of modal learning.[10] Philosophers,
however, for mysterious reasons, find it necessary to try to go beyond these modes of experience to grasp the whole unmodified, the
whole as whole.

Even if this philosophic effort cannot come to completion, as
Oakeshott thinks it cannot, the result of the effort is to experience
the full weight of the discrepancy between that which would satisfy
the philosophical quest and all the images of satisfaction offered by
the various modal interpretations of the whole. The philosopher
as such could never thereafter be satisfied by these substitutes, nor
find a way to escape them altogether. The philosopher is caught
between the insufficient and the infinitely removed. He is no longer
simply a practitioner within one of the limited modes, nor is he
able to claim satisfactory achievement of something better.

There is a gulf between the philosopher's understanding of the
world and the understandings of others even though they are
bound together in the endless task of self-understanding which
is the dispensation of all humanity in all times and places. This
condition does not, for Oakeshott, put the philosopher in a super-

---

[9] 'Now, in the first place, whatever else a mode of experience, a divergence from the
concrete purpose in experience, may escape, it cannot escape from the world of experience
itself. A mode of experience is defective, not because it has ceased to be experience or has
abandoned the proper criterion of experience, but because it no longer attempts to satisfy
that criterion in full.' *Experience and its Modes*, p. 71.

[10] A 'mode' of experience is not merely a 'perspective' on things. A mode is a disciplined, if ultimately arbitrarily bounded, account of experience proceeding from certain
assumptions about the way in which the world is to be explained and which develops over
time peculiar methods of inquiry that will create a body of organized knowledge and
identifiable manners of conduct that will portray our world of experience as, implicitly, the
practitioners learn to expect the world to look: the historian's past, the scientist's nature,
the politician's project for progress, the poet's world of images, the composer's melodies.
Nevertheless, in the course of things the various modes of experience will influence the
casual perspectives people generally hold. Modes tend to exclusivity, perspectives may be
more casual and amiable. And, of course, perspectives can coexist among practitioners
within modes.

8

ior position; it does put him in a peculiar position, not easily appreciated by those not similarly entangled.[11]

In the meantime, the practitioners of the various modes of experience get on with the business of giving their respective lines of thought greater organizational clarity in terms of more or less unquestioned postulates or assumptions; of simplifying their work in the form of manuals and textbooks so that their activity can be taught to initiates who will carry it on. The attraction of this lies in the sense of completion and security, of specifiable purpose, imparted to the practitioner. Not surprisingly, then, practitioners greet the scepticism of the philosopher, who calls attention to the limits of a mode of experience, without enthusiasm.

The philosopher's interest in a mode of experience – scientific experimentation, historical research, writing poetry, political action – extends to exploring and stating its interior logic in a mood of detachment from it. The philosopher's business is neither to praise nor to blame, but to reveal. In the course of mapping this intellectual terrain, he also reveals where features of experience have been set aside, left unaccounted for, as the price of achieving modal coherency. The philosopher potentially forces the practitioners of an activity to become self-conscious, putting them on the road to becoming self-critical where they may undergo the philosopher's own experience of puzzlement.

This philosophic intervention does not in any obvious way add to the capacity of practitioners to practice their activity; anything the philosopher discovers as an organizing standard is already implicit within it. He certainly does not provide an extrinsic goal or ulterior purpose to anchor the activity in question. Understanding is an end in itself. It is sought for its own sake, as understanding without limits. What the philosopher's intervention does do, whether by design or not, is to convict an activity of abstraction from the whole in its very effort to be the whole. Philosophic intervention, in short, raises the spectre of incoherency, and hence of insecurity, where coherency and security had been thought to be

[11] The philosopher sees an identity 'not as a verdict to be accepted but as an invitation to interrogate it . . .', ultimately by 'seeking to understand them in terms of their postulates; that is, in terms of their conditions'. And 'a theorist is not provoked to this enterprise by his recognition of identities as compositions of characteristics (these he already understands, perhaps as well as they may be understood), but by what in such identities he does not yet understand; namely, their conditionality. In turning his critical attention to this conditionality he is realeased from the prison of his current understanding . . .' *On Human Conduct*, pp. 8–9. The theoretical endeavour implies unconditional knowing as its object, but it appears that there is no end to the conditional platforms of understanding to be investigated.

9

possible. The philosopher's refusal to credit the certainty that the practitioners thought they had found opens the whole enterprise to doubt, potentially infecting them with the philosopher's sceptical disease.[12]

This brings before us the inevitable conflict between philosophers and everyone else which is familiar to all readers of philosophy. Here, indeed, is Oakeshott's interpretation of Plato's allegory of the cave: philosophy leads necessarily to scepticism about all human claims to have understood, including those that the philosopher may be tempted to make for himself.[13] Every modal interpretation of experience is reductionist in seeking to complete itself by explaining all experience in terms of its own postulates of interpretation.

In following this Socratic–Platonic style of investigation which leads towards scepticism about any claims of adequacy by a mode of experience, Oakeshott finds no warrant for any particular mode to dominate or define human existence. Thus Oakeshott's essays on education, as on every subject, bring out the romance of possibility which lurks in the drab corners of practical life. For him, education can counter the inertial tendencies that obscure the multiplicity of possibilities in human existence.

It is not the business of those devoted to art, literature and philosophy to come out of a retreat, bringing with them some superior wisdom; to be free from the world – which also means they must acknowledge the world's self-sufficiency – is the condition of their contribution. Oakeshott's scepticism is thus quite direct but in the manner of friendly detachment, not of hostility. He lets the scepticism of philosophical reflection emerge as the means of eliciting openness to the possibilities of human existence as may be discovered by individuals on their own, not as laid down by him or anyone else. The responsibility of self-definition is an ordeal of consciousness which human beings cannot escape, but it is also a great adventure which Oakeshott takes as seriously as if it were the soul ascending.

[12] 'What distinguishes philosophy from all other experience is the explicit attempt to achieve what is finally satisfactory in experience. If it fails to achieve this, then it fails to achieve anything it can recognize as an achievement. And this at once differentiates it from an abstract world of experience such as the world of history, of science or of practce. These, though they fail to achieve what is satisfactory in experience, fail because they achieve something else – a specific degree of what is satisfactory. Thus, it is not in virtue of its actual achievement that an experience may be called philosophical; rather, philosophy should be regarded as the determination to be satisfied only with a completely coherent world of experience.' *Experience and its Modes*, p. 347.
[13] See Oakeshott's discussion of this point in *On Human Conduct*, p. 27; and *Rationalism in Politics*, p. 224, footnote 1 and *passim*.

INTRODUCTION

Practical engagements define life as a series of problems to be solved. Thinking in practical terms can easily make us blind to the thought that, because we are mortal beings, life cannot be transformed into a 'problem' with a 'solution'. Life cannot be manipulated to deliver a succession of predictable satisfactions. The human condition is a predicament, not an itinerary.

The engagements of the contemplative, the poet, the philosopher, the scientist who seeks to understand nature's structure, the historian who is in love with the past for its own sake, are not marginal but crucial in appreciating what it means to be human. At the furthest reaches from practicality, Oakeshott celebrates the poetic impulse and contemplative delight: 'images in contemplation are merely present; they provoke neither speculation nor inquiry about the occasion or conditions of their appearing but only delight in their having appeared.'[14]

The quiet but assured appraisal that emerges in these essays would have suggested not so long ago a sense of providential order that here is not named. This is consistent with Oakeshott's own admission of the consequences of his philosophical scepticism. To invoke a supportive foundation would be only to invoke an individual self-understanding which could easily divert attention from the experience of teaching and learning itself. It is to the description of the experience that he constantly turns.

He does so because, whatever metaphysical ground one might introduce in order to explain the experience, it is the acknowledgement of the experience itself which can be shared and delineated through a conversation among those who have enjoyed it, despite disagreements that might arise about where the experience comes from or where it may lead. Conversation of this sort expresses for Oakeshott the central character of human existence – the civility of the agreement to disagree – and thus also the importance for us of the institutions of teaching and learning, the places where conversationality is explicitly given priority. It is when teaching and learning allow us to forget for a while to be preoccupied with ulterior goals and purposes that they fulfill the peculiarly human desire for self-understanding which gives rise to them.

If philosophical investigation is always for the purpose of clarifying the distinguishing features of an activity – the features which set it apart as identifiably not anything else but itself – this is no less the task of philosophy when it turns its attention to understand-

---

[14] 'The Voice of Poetry in the Conversation of Mankind', *Rationalism in Politics*, (London: Methuen & Co Ltd, 1962) p. 217.

THE VOICE OF LIBERAL LEARNING

ing teaching and learning. Every consideration that imperils the clarity of our vision of the thing to be understood is suspicious.

Oakeshott's fundamental cheerfulness as a sceptical philosopher derives from his awareness that nothing is being ruled in or out. The philosopher is not a judge in a court of last resort; humanity requires no such judge. The task of clarifying is the philosophic way of inviting a conversational response from others. It does not seek to dictate.

Liberation of the mind for such conversation is also its elevation. Teaching and learning are bulwarks against superficiality and routine, which preoccupation with practical affairs often induces. Elevation here does not imply any desire for rule by cultural arbiters. Rather, the hope is to move from thinking in terms of protection of our intellectual resources to rejuvenating them by enjoying them. Although practical discourse often dwells on protecting society, Oakeshott proposes that the strength of a civilization derives from the capacity for continual self-recreation or renewal.

Practical life cannot preclude preoccupation with specific goals and plans, interminable debates over means and ends. There are elements of conversationality in the day-to-day practicalities of existence to be sure, but seldom the chance for creating an atmosphere of continual conversation for its own sake, a situation in which little must be resolved.

The word 'conversation' evokes the manner of the 'conversationalist', taken by Oakeshoot as one who is the agent of a flow of sympathy, not the utterer of a truth. The conversationalist is neither a lawgiver nor a prophet, much less a revolutionary reformer choosing to live for a future age. At any rate, if an entrant to a place of learning is inclined to be any of these things, he should know enough to check his guns at the door.

The philosopher will prove an engaging conversationalist, provided that he does not lose a healthy sense of his own unimportance. But tension threatens, given the depressing effect when the philosopher is obliged to say

> men sail a boundless and bottomless sea; there is neither harbour for shelter nor floor for anchorage, neither starting-place nor appointed destination. The enterprise is to keep afloat on an even keel; the sea is both friend and enemy; and the seamanship consists in using the resources of a traditional manner of behaviour in order to make a friend of every hostile occasion.[15]

[15] 'Political Education', see pp. 149–50.

INTRODUCTION

What may depress people of affairs when expressed in this way may also inspire when it is put differently:

> In conversation, 'facts' appear only to be resolved once more into the possibilities from which they were made; 'certainties' are shown to be combustible, not by being brought into contact with other 'certainties' or with doubts, but by being kindled by the presence of ideas of another order; approximations are revealed between notions normally remote from one another. Thoughts of different species take wing and play round one another, responding to each other's movements and provoking one another to fresh exertions. Nobody asks where they have come from or on what authority they are present; nobody cares what will become of them when they have played their part. There is no symposiarch or arbiter; not even a doorkeeper to examine credentials. Every entrant is taken at its face-value and everything is permitted which can get itself accepted into the flow of speculation. And voices which speak in conversation do not compose a hierarchy. Conversation is not an enterprise designed to yield an extrinsic profit, a contest where a winner gets a prize, nor is it an activity of/exegesis? It is an unrehearsed intellectual adventure. It is with conversation as with gambling, its significance lies neither in winning nor in losing, but in wagering.[16]

These two passages suggest 'formality' rather than 'agenda'. There is a mode of conduct appropriate to the conversation of scholars, teachers and students which does not specify a hierarchy of learning and hence no 'symposiarch' or arbiter of the ultimate content of learning. This conduct includes the facility Hirsch denotes as 'cultural literacy', but also much more. Moreover, in its opposition to hierarchy we see a quiet refusal to allow learning and teaching to be captured by moralists who would constrain the conversation in accordance with a specific vision of what a human being should or must become.

One can see that all of Oakeshott's philosophical reflections lead away from constraints in teaching and learning on self-interpretation as much as they lead away from sociological or psychological reductions. And this distinguishes him sharply from such writers as Allan Bloom, who, not without reason, fears that the chaotic diversity of goings-on in the modern university is dangerous to the moral health of students and of a civilization whose success he equates with American success. Undoubtedly there are

---

[16] 'The Voice of Poetry in the Conversation of Mankind', *Rationalism in Politics*, p. 198.

grave moral dangers, and Oakeshott would not be unsympathetic to Bloom's catalogue of the vulgarities of modern culture. But their respective prescriptions for the diseases of the soul (Oakeshott would say misinterpretations) are strikingly different. Oakeshott's quiet voice of refusal to compromise the idea of education, reflecting his dispositionally stoic capacity to keep his eye on the idea of teaching and learning amidst the rubbish, is to be contrasted with the agonized lament that reveals Bloom's alienation from a modernity that he understands as Rousseau and Nietzsche understood it.[17]

There can be no doubt that Bloom's call to construct a strategy for preserving our civilization rests on persuading us that we are encountering a unique moment of threat (and opportunity) in which it is clear what needs to be said. Oakeshott characteristically resists all apocalyptic formulations, seeing in them recipes for suspending conversationality in favour of a politicizing counter-revolution that will define education as the carrying on of war by other means. This, for Oakeshott, is an interpretative response to contingent circumstances. There is no immediate way to reconcile these points of interpretative difference, but that gives all the more reason to reflect on what each voice has to say – to converse.

Consider again Oakeshott's two aforementioned remarks, often quoted by Oakeshott's readers, but seldom put side by side: the former establishes the austere limits of human existence; the latter praises what humanity can do for itself. Here we see the rhythm of thought inspired by Oakeshott's devoted reading of the arguments of Thomas Hobbes.

Like Hobbes, Oakeshott couples a constant remembrance of the reasons for mankind to be humble, rather than proud, with a striking belief in the capacity of men so instructed to create a world for themselves in which there is much to delight in: we need political authority; we do not need symposiarchs or cultural arbiters, nor, finally, prophets.

The second passage describes exchanges more likely to be observed unmistakably and concretely in a 'place of learning' than anywhere else. It is in colleges and universites at their best that

---

[17] Allan Bloom, *The Closing of the American Mind: How Higher Education Has Failed Democracy and Impoverished the Souls of Today's Students* (New York: Simon & Schuster, 1987). Bloom ends his book by saying: 'This is the American moment in world history, the one for which we shall be forever judged. Just as in politics the responsibility for the fate of freedom in the world devolved upon our regime, so the fate of philosophy in the world has devolved upon our universities, and the two are related as they have never been before. The gravity of our given task is great, and it is very much in doubt how the future will judge our stewardship.' p. 382.

Oakeshott would expect to renew the confidence that human intelligence can continue to use the resources of its history, that intelligence is not to be exhausted. It is not the case that the more intelligence is used, the more it will be used up. Nor is it the case that there is nothing to discuss when no purpose or unifying goal has been settled upon. Nor is it even the case that the great conversation need ever be redeemed by settling purposes and goals. Indeed, it is a responsibility simply to embody and exemplify the possibilities of the conversational relationship in a world ever ready to ignore them.

Most of us will remain at best briefly in such a place; but the experience of it can leaven our lives even while far away in the world of getting and spending. This cannot be captured by 'cultural literacy' (although those who carry the experience undoubtedly will be 'culturally literate'), nor is it insured by the imposition of any particular hierarchy of textual resources (although liberally educated people will surely display connoisseurship in what they choose to pursue). Supposing that ours is not the eschatological moment, does that alter the commitment? And is the nature of the commitment made any clearer by presenting it in desperate terms? Oakeshott will consistently answer no to these questions, seeing that this approach must, however gripping, reinsert an extrinsic goal or ulterior purpose as the principal motive to teaching and learning.

From these observations we may draw both energy to carry on and a sober understanding of the perpetuity of the human condition: tradition, upon which we must rely, 'is not susceptible of the distinction between essence and accident, knowledge of it is unavoidably knowledge of its detail; and this imparts to the knowledgeable *an attitude of energetic sobriety*'. Intimacy with a manner of living indicates how we may conduct ourselves but not a direction in which we are required to go. Inspiration comes from 'thinkers and statesmen who knew which way to turn their feet without knowing anything about a final destination'.[18]

Oakeshott's disposition is to conserve, but it is non-programmatic. What, above all, is to be conserved is clarity of vision about the distinguishing features of the distinctive human endeavours. No obvious generalizations about public policies or programs may be drawn from what the philosopher knows. He is not in business to dictate when any idea's time has come, and when it has gone; he seeks, rather, to transcend such vulgarities. The effect on policy

[18] 'Political Education', see p. 153. Italics added.

will be at most indirect, and very likely inadvertent. Oakeshott has, for example, consistently and unequivocally resisted the 'crisis mentality' of our time which has infected academic institutions with a powerful urge to claim competence to lead the world, to assess the world's successes and failures, to prophesy a destination.

If teaching and learning foster anything, it is intellectual and emotional maturity: finding a way to be at home in the world. The movement of Oakeshott's thought parallels that of Montaigne: the world's order is complicated by each entry of a new human being. The disharmonizing effect is charming in youth but it must be succeeded by reflective acknowledgement of the world's vast variety and our incapacity to find an expression of it that is all-encompassing.

There is no rule to enforce this acknowledgement upon us. We may face it with more or less grace; but it is the victory of finding the days of age equal to the days of youth which qualifies us for facing up to practicality, for persevering, for the not always exhilarating task of attending to the arrangements of our society with each other.

It is above all the calling of the teacher who has remained a learner to discover how to be at home in the world when forever conversing with the exuberant young: to be both old and young at once. In this Socrates has always been our exemplar and, to his students, Michael Oakeshott is his current embodiment.

A PLACE OF LEARNING

1975

Un début dans la vie humaine. Paul Valéry

We are concerned with ourselves and what we may be said to know about ourselves. This comes to us, first, in what purports to be information of various sorts. We are informed, for example, that human beings are the most intricate of living organisms, that they have evolved over millions of years from less complicated organizations of chemical constituents, that each is endowed with an inherited genetic character, subject to modification, which by means of complex processes governs its movements, and that these movements are continuously directed to the self-maintenance of the organism and to the survival of the species. Alternatively, human beings are alleged to be sentient creatures all of whose movements and utterances are expressions of a desire for pleasure and aversion from pain. We are told, further, that Man was cre-

Editorial note: First presented at Colorado College as the Abbott Memorial Lecture in the Social Sciences on the occasion of the College's Centennial, September 1974. These were Michael Oakeshott's opening words: 'I have crossed half the world to find myelf in familiar surroundings: a place of learning. The occasion is a cheerful one: the celebration of the centenary of your foundation, and I hope you will not think me patronizing if I first express my admiration for you and all others who, through the centuries, sailing under the flag of the Liberal Arts, have, with becoming humility, summoned succeeding generations to the enjoyment of their human inheritance. But it is an occasion also for reflection. And I have been honoured with an invitation to say something about the educational engagement which you and others have undertaken and to reconsider this adventure in relation to present circumstances. This is a large order, and you will forgive me if I respond to it only in part. Education is a transaction between teachers and learners, but I shall be concerned only with learners, with what there is to be learned and (in the first place) with learning as the distinguishing mark of a human being. A man is what he learns to become: this is the human condition.'

ated by God, bidden to people the earth, endowed with an un-
limited right to exploit its resources and directed not to be idle.
And a human being has been said to be an immortal soul of
unknown destiny lodged for a time in a mortal body. And so on.

Now, each of these statements about human beings is capable
of elaboration in which its meaning may become clearer, thus
allowing us to consider it from the point of view of whatever truth
or error it may contain. They may all turn out to be (in some
sense) true, or they may all be convicted of some error or obscurity.
But with conclusions of this sort we are not now concerned. What
concerns us is that each is itself a human utterance expressing a
human understanding of the character of a human being, and
that the capacity to make such utterances, whether they be true or
false, itself postulates a man who is something besides what these,
or any other such statements, allege him to be. They postulate
what I shall call a 'free' man.

A human being may become 'free' in many different respects,
and I shall suggest later that becoming educated is itself an emancipation; and human beings may also achieve various other degrees
of what may be 'autonomy'; but I am concerned now with the
'freedom' (so to call it) of which a human being cannot divest himself or be deprived without temporarily or permanently ceasing to
be human.

What, then, are we to understand by this 'freedom' inherent in
being a human and postulated in his capacity to make statements
about himself? It is often identified with his having what is called
a 'free will'. This is usually the case when what is being considered
is the kind of utterance we call an action. But it is not a very
satisfactory way of speaking. It is difficult to imagine what an 'un-
free' will would be. If what is being said is that human actions and
utterances, properly speaking, are 'free' because they are willed
(that is, because they are the outcomes of desires and understand-
able only in terms of wants), then we are left with the question:
in virtue of what must desiring be considered necessarily to be a
'free' activity? Perhaps this inherent human 'freedom', exhibited
when a man makes or entertains statements about himself, is
better identified in terms of his ability to understand, or (of course)
misunderstand, himself. He is sometimes said to have this ability
in virtue of having, or being, a mind as well as a body. We must,
however, be careful how we construe this distinction. What it
distinguishes is not two things but, on the one hand, a process or
organization of processes (the outcome of which is, for example,
blue eyes or genetic resistance to malaria), and on the other hand

the ability to understand such a process in terms of its regularities, to identify the substances involved and to discern how they are related to one another.

In short, there is an important distinction here between a chemical process and a biochemist understanding and explaining (well or ill) what is going on in a chemical process. For mind is not itself a chemical process, nor is it a mysterious x left over, unexplained, after the biochemist has reached the end of his chemical explanation; it is what does the explaining. A geneticist, for example, cannot be merely a clerk who records the utterances of his own genes; such a record would not constitute a contribution to a science of genetics, and in any case genes are incapable of such utterances about themselves; they can make only blue eyes or a propensity to live a long time. Mind, here, is the intelligent activity in which a man may understand and explain processes which cannot understand and explain themselves.

But this is only one aspect of the matter. Intelligence is not merely concerned to understand physiological processes. Mind is made of perceptions, recognitions, thoughts of all kinds; of emotions, sentiments, affections, deliberations and purposes, and of actions which are responses to what is understood to be going on. It is the author not only of the intelligible world in which a human being lives but also of his self-conscious relationship to that world, a self-consciousness which may rise to the condition of a self-understanding. This inherent 'freedom' of a human being lies not only in his ability to make statements expressing his understanding of himself, but also in the world's being for him what he understands it to be, and in his being what he understands himself to be. A human being is 'free', not because he has 'free will', but because he is *in* himself what he is *for* himself.

This reading of the human condition is familiar enough. It is embedded in the epic and dramatic literatures of the Western world and in the writings of historians: this is how human beings appear in Homer, in the sagas of Scandinavia, in Shakespeare and Racine, in Livy and in Gibbon. Not even the driest of modern behaviourists or the most blinkered neurobiologist is able wholly to reject it without rejecting himself. There have been times when this reading of human character was not only accepted but was embraced with enthusiasm. It was recognized as a glorious distinction to be welcomed, to be explored, cultivated and enjoyed; it was said to constitute the dignity of man. But, even then, this condition of being intelligent was seen to carry with it a penalty: the possibility of being wise entails the possibility of being stupid. Moreover, such a man is unavoidably responsible for his thoughts, utterances and actions. He cannot plead that his thoughts are caused by his inherited genetic character because thoughts have reasons and not causes and these reasons are other thoughts. He cannot plead that his utterances are not his own but are words put into his mouth by a god or that they are merely electrical discharges of his brain: they have meanings for which he is responsible and are judged in terms of whether or not they make sense. He cannot plead that his actions are not his own but are merely the outcomes of irresponsible biological urges, like the branches thrown out by a tree: these actions also have meanings and are chosen responses to understood situations.

Further, because this 'freedom' inherent in the human condition is not gratuitous and has to be paid for in responsibility, it has been viewed with misgivings and even counted a misery to be escaped, if only escape were possible. How much less burdensome to be incapable of error, of stupidity, of hatred and of wrongdoing, even if this meant the surrender of truth, wisdom, love and virtue. But it is impossible. The very contemplation of such an escape announces its impossibility: only mind can regret having to think. Instead of deploring our condition we would be better employed considering exactly what price we pay for our unsought and inescapable 'freedom'.

I have called this price 'responsibility', although the word has an inappropriate moral overtone. It suggests that we might refuse to pay for the freedom inherent in intelligent activity and that this refusal would somehow be a dereliction of duty. However, it would be merely a failure to recognize a necessary condition. What distinguishes a human being, indeed what constitutes a human being, is not merely his having to think, but his thoughts, his beliefs, doubts, understandings, his awareness of his own ignorance, his wants, preferences, choices, sentiments, emotions, purposes and his expression of them in utterances or actions which have meanings; and the necessary condition of all or any of this is that he must have *learned* it. The price of the intelligent activity which constitutes being human is learning. When the human condition is said to be burdensome what is being pointed to is not the mere necessity of having to think, to speak and to act (instead of merely *being* like a stone, or growing like a tree) but the impossibility of thinking or feeling without having slowly and often painfully learned to think something. The freedom of a human being inheres in his thoughts and his emotions having had to be learned; for learning is something which each of us must do and can only do for ourselves.

This inseparability of learning and being human is central to our understanding of ourselves. It means that none of us is born human; each is what he learns to become. It means that what characterizes a man is what he has actually learned to perceive, to think and to do, and that the important differences between human beings are differences in respect of what they have actually learned. There is little doubt that our ability to learn has increased during the last million years or so, and that this ability is greater at some periods of our individual lives than at others. Perhaps also there are some genetic differences in our several abilities to learn. The human significances of these changes and differences, however, lies only in their reflection in what a man has actually learned to think, to imagine and to do; for this is what he is. It means, also that these differences are not merely those of more or of less success in learning, of better or worse achievements in becoming human, but are also incommensurable differences of human individuality. In short, this connection between learning and being human means that each man is his own self-enacted 'history'; and the expression 'human nature' stands only for our common and inescapable engagement: to become by learning.

But what is this engagement I have called 'learning' in which alone we may become human? Let me notice, first, an account of the matter which, whatever its shortcomings, is at least clear. A biologist will tell us that a living organism (an octopus, for example) exists in relation to its environment. The organism is a continuously changing chemical structure sensitive to its circumstances and equipped to react to the stimulus of its surroundings. Its reactions are movements, not always successful, favouring its survival. The inputs it receives from its environment are not uniform or necessarily favourable, and in order to survive the organism must be versatile in its reaction. Indeed, it is equipped with mechanisms which favour and record for future use successful or 'correct' reactions and suppress or disfavour those which have been unsuccessful or 'incorrect'. This process in which an organism adapts itself and records its reactions to its environment is called 'learning'; indeed, it is spoken of as a process of acquiring, storing and retrieving useful information, and in a human being it is said to be only more versatile than in an octopus.

We need not question this account of metabolic and evolutionary change, rich in anthropomorphic analogy though it be. Nor need we doubt that some such process goes on in the early days of our postnatal existence. Yet clearly the learning in which we may become human is very different from this process of organic adaptation to circumstances. Indeed, the latter is not a recognizable description of the learning by means of which the biologist himself came to discern and to understand the organic process. Is Dr. Watson's discovery of the helical structure of DNA molecules properly to be described as itself a chemical reaction to an environmental input which promoted his biological survival?

The learning we are concerned with is a self-conscious engagement. It is not an induced reaction to a fortuitous environmental pressure but a self-imposed task inspired by the intimations of what there is to learn (that is, by awareness of our own ignorance) and by a wish to understand. Human learning is a reflective engagement in which what is learned is not merely a detached fragment of information but is understood or misunderstood and is expressed in words which have meanings. It has nothing to do with organic survival and much of it has little to do even with that selective 'getting on in the world' which is the human counterpart of organic homeostasis; it is concerned with perceptions, ideas, beliefs, emotions, sensibilities, recognitions, discriminations, theorems and with all that goes to constitute a human condition.

In these respects, human learning is distinguished also from other experiences, or alleged experiences, with which it is sometimes confused. Human learning is not acquiring habits or being trained to perform tricks or functions; it is acquiring something that you can use because you understand it. Further, the feelings of euphoria, of illumination or of depression which are induced by drugs, by flashing lights or by electrical currents are no more learned than the unconsciousness induced by an anaesthetic, and they are no more significant; they make no contribution whatever to the achievement of a human condition. Indeed, in so far as they suggest that this condition can be acquired by chemical stimulus or by magic they obstruct the arduous self-conscious engagement of learning in which alone we may become human. Being bewitched is not learning. Nor is learning a teleological process in which a suppositious seed of *humanitas* in each of us grows and realizes or develops what is already potential in it. The nearest we can get to what may be called a distinguishing 'natural' human equipment is self-consciousness; that, too, however is learned, although it begins to be learned very early in our individual lives. And while self-consciousness is the condition of all human intellectual and imaginative achievement, the vast variety of these achievements cannot be said to be potential in it.

Let me sum up this part of what I have to say. A human life is not a process in which a living organism grows to maturity, succeeds in accommodating itself to its surroundings or perishes.

It is, in the first place, an adventure in which an individual consciousness confronts the world he inhabits, responds to what Henry James called 'the ordeal of consciousness', and thus enacts and discloses himself. This engagement is an adventure in a precise sense. It has no pre-ordained course to follow: with every thought and action a human being lets go a mooring and puts out to sea on a self-chosen but largely unforeseen course. It has no pre-ordained destination: there is no substantive perfect man or human life upon which he may model his conduct. It is a predicament, not a journey. A human being is a 'history' and he makes this 'history' for himself out of his responses to the vicissitudes he encounters. The world he inhabits is composed not of 'things', but of occurrences, which he is aware of in terms of what they mean to him and to which he must respond in terms of what he understands them to be.[1] Some of these occurrences he learns to recognize as expressions of human thoughts and emotions – stories, poems, works of art, musical compositions, landscapes, human actions, utterances and gestures, religious beliefs, enquiries, sciences, procedures, practices and other artefacts of all sorts, which again, he is aware of only in terms of his understanding of them. Others he learns to recognize as intelligent persons whom he is aware of in terms of who and what he understands them to be, and to whom he is related in terms of transactions and utterances which have meanings and may be understood or misunderstood. In short, he inhabits a wholly human world, not because it contains nothing but human beings and their artefacts, but because everything in it is *known* to him in terms of what it *means* to him. A human being is condemned to be a learner because meanings have to be learned. Whatever a man thinks or says or does is unavoidably what he has learned (well or ill) to think, to say or to do. Even a human death is something learned.

2

For a human being, then, learning is a lifelong engagement; the world he inhabits is a place of learning. But, further, human beings, in so far as they have understood their condition, have always recognized special places, occasions and circumstances de-

[1] Moreover, human beings, although they do not have the god-like power to confer self-consciousness where it is absent, do have the power to individualize and endow into historical life things and creatures which are not themselves historical: horses, dogs, trees.

liberately designed for and devoted to learning, the most notable of which are the human family, school and university. The human family (whatever form it may take) is a practice devised, not for the procreation of children, nor merely for their protection, but for the early education of newcomers to the human scene: it recognizes that learning begins slowly and takes time. School and university are unmistakable; they are successive stages in this deliberate engagement to learn, and it is with these that we are concerned.

The distinctive feature of such a special place of learning is, first, that those who occupy it are recognized and recognize themselves pre-eminently as learners, although they may be much else besides. Secondly, in it learning is a declared engagement to learn something in particular. Those who occupy it are not merely 'growing up', and they are not there merely to 'improve their minds' or to 'learn to think'; such unspecified activities are as impossible as an orchestra that plays no music in particular. Further, what is to be learned in such a place does not present itself by chance or arise circumstantially out of whatever may happen to be going on; it is recognized as a specified task to be undertaken and pursued with attention, patience and determination, the learner being aware of what he is doing. And thirdly, learning here is not a limited undertaking in which what is learned is learned merely up to the point where it can be put to some extrinsic use; learning itself is the engagement and it has its own standards of achievement and excellence. Consequently, what is special about such a place or circumstance is its seclusion, its detachment from what Hegel called the *hic et munc*, the here and now, of current living.

Each of us is born in a corner of the earth and at a particular moment in historic time, lapped round with locality. But school and university are places apart where a declared learner is emancipated from the limitations of his local circumstances and from the wants he may happen to have acquired, and is moved by intimations of what he has never yet dreamed. He finds himself invited to pursue satisfactions he has never yet imagined or wished for. They are, then, sheltered places where excellences may be heard because the din of local partialities is no more than a distant rumble. They are places where a learner is initiated into what there is to be learned.

But what is there for a human being to learn? A large part of human conduct is, and always has been, concerned with exploiting the resources of the earth for the satisfaction of human wants, and much of human learning is concerned, directly or indirectly, with this endlessly proliferating intelligent engagement. This certainly is genuine learning. An otter may be equipped with what, for want of a better word, we call an instinct which enables it to catch fish, a beaver in response to some biological urge may build a dam and an eagle may swoop down and carry off a lamb; but a fisherman must learn to catch fish and he learns to do so well or ill and with a variety of techniques, the engineers who designed and built the Boulder Dam were equipped with something more than a biological urge, and to breed sheep for meat or wool is an art that has to be learned. In respect of being concerned to exploit the resources of the earth a current human being is, then, an inheritor of a vast variety of instrumental skills and practices which have to be learned if they are to yield the satisfactions they are designed to yield. Moreover, the inventor and the user of these skills and practices is not Man or Society; each is the discovery or invention of assignable men, a Prometheus, a Vulcan, a Bessemer or an Edison. It is not Man or some abstraction called 'medical science' which cures the sick; it is an individual doctor who has himself learned his art from some assignable teachers. There is no such thing as 'social learning' or 'collective understanding'. The arts and practices we share with one another are nowhere to be found save in the understandings of living, individual adepts who have learned them.

And further, the satisfaction of human wants is pursued in transactions between human beings in which they compete or co-operate with one another. To seek the satisfaction of a want is to enter into relationships with other human beings. This human association is not the interaction of the components of a process, nor is it an unspecified gregariousness or sociability; it is made up of a variety of different kinds of relationships, each a specific practice whose conditions must be learned and understood if its advantages are to be enjoyed. Incomparably, the most useful of these relationships is that which subsists between those who speak a common language in which to communicate their wants and to conduct the bargains in which they may be satisfied. Such a language, like all other conditions of human association, has to be learned.

To be human, to have wants and to try to satisfy them, is, then, to have the use of particular skills, instrumental practices and relationships. There is no action which is not a subscription to some art, and utterance is impossible without a language. These skills, practices and relationships have to be learned. Since this learning, so far as it goes, is genuine and may be extensive, it is no surprise that there should be special places devoted to it, each concerned to initiate learners into some particular instrumental art or practice and often equipped with the opportunity of 'learning on the job', as it is called: medical schools, law schools, language schools, schools of journalism or photography, schools where one may learn to cook, to drive an automobile or to run a bassoon factory, and even polytechnics where a variety of such instrumental skills may be learned.

There is much more that might be said about this activity of exploiting the earth, of the arts and relationships used in the satisfaction of human wants and the learning these entail. It is certainly genuine learning, although the special places devoted to it are appropriately limited in their aims and in their seclusion from considerations of utility. To learn an instrumental art is not merely being trained to perform a trick; it entails understanding what you are doing. And learning a practice is not merely acquiring a mechanical contrivance and knowing how to work it. A human art is never fixed and finished; it has to be used and it is continuously modified in use. Even using a language to communicate wants is itself an inventive engagement. But I do not propose to explore further this engagement in learning; there is something more important for us to consider. We catch a glimpse of it when we recognize that choosing wants to satisfy is also something that has to be learned and that the conditions to be subscribed to in making such choices are not the terms of the instrumental arts and practices in which chosen wants may be conveniently satisfied. It is never enough to say of a human want: 'I know how to satisfy it and I have the power to do so'. There is always something else to consider. But what comes into view is not merely an extension of the field of instrumental learning but an altogether different engagement of critical self-understanding in which we relate ourselves, not to our inheritance of instrumental arts, but to the continuous intellectual adventure in which human beings have sought to identify and to understand themselves.

To recognize oneself in terms of one's wants, to recognize the world as material to be shaped and used in satisfying wants, to recognize others as competitors or co-operators in this enterprise and to recognize our inheritance of arts and practices, including a common language, as valuable instruments for satisfying wants – all this is, unquestionably, *a* self-understanding. It gives *an* answer to the question, who am I? And indeed there are some who would persuade us that this is all we know or can know about ourselves and that all other thoughts human beings have had about themselves and the world are idle fancies and all other relationships are shadowy reflections of this relationship. But they refute themselves. In purporting to make a true statement about human beings and their relationships they identify themselves as something other than mere seekers after contingent satisfactions; they assume a relationship between themselves and those whom they address which is not that of exploiters of the resources of the earch but that of persons capable of considering the truth or falsehood of a theorem.[2]

But be that how it may, it is unquestionable that human beings, without denying their identities as exploiters of the resources of the earth, have always thought of themselves as something other than this and that they have been tireless in their explorations of these other identities. They have engaged in manifold activities other than this – adventures of intellectual enquiry, of moral discrimination and of emotional and imaginative insight; they have explored a vast variety of relationships other than this – moral, intellectual, emotional, civil; and they have perceived, dimly or clearly, that this identity as exploiters of the resources of the earth is not only evanescent and insubstantial when set beside those others but is itself conditional upon them. They have recognized that these understandings of themselves, and these valuations of occurrences, like everything else human, are themselves human inventions and can be enjoyed only in learning. Even in the most difficult circumstances, overwhelmed by the exigencies of the moment (life in the covered wagon, for example), they have carried these identities with them and imparted them to their children if only in songs and stories. Whenever opportunity has occurred they have set aside special places and occasions devoted to this learning, and until recently schools and universities were just such places of learning, sheltered enough from the demands of utility to be undistracted in their concern with these adventures and expressions of human self-understanding.

3

This, then, is what we are concerned with: adventures in human self-understanding. Not the bare protestation that a human being is

---

[2] When Francis Bacon identified human beings as exploiters of the resources of the earth and language as a means of communicating information about wants he added that this identity had been imposed upon us by God – thus identifying human beings *also* in relation to God. Even Karl Marx, inconsistently, recognized something called 'scientific' enquiry independent of the current conditions of productive undertaking.

a self-conscious, reflective intelligence and that he does not live by bread alone, but the actual enquiries, utterances and actions in which human beings have expressed their understanding of the human condition. This is the stuff of what has come to be called a 'liberal' education – 'liberal' because it is liberated from the distracting business of satisfying contingent wants.

But why should we be concerned with it? If it purported to provide reliable information about 'human nature' our concern would be intelligible. But it does not. There is no such thing as 'human nature'; there are only men, women, and children responding gaily or reluctantly, reflectively or not so reflectively, to the ordeal of consciousness, who exist only in terms of their self-understandings. Nor is being human itself a special instrumental skill like that of an electrical engineer. And if our concern is with human self-understanding, why all this paraphernalia of learning? Is this not something we each do for ourselves? Yes, humanly each of us is self-made; but not out of nothing, and not by the light of nature. The world is full of home-made human beings, but they are rickety constructions of impulses ready to fall apart in what is called an 'identity crisis'. Being human is an historic adventure which has been going on since the earth rose out of the sea, and we are concerned with this paraphernalia of learning because it is the only way we have of participating in this adventure. The ancient Greek exhortation, Know Thyself, meant *learn* to know thyself. It was not an exhortation to buy a book on psychology and study it; it meant, contemplate and learn from what men, from time to time, have made of this engagement of learning to be a man.

Human self-understanding is, then, inseparable from learning to participate in what is called a 'culture'. It is useful to have a word which stands for the whole of what an associated set of human beings have created for themselves beyond the evanescent satisfaction of their wants, but we must not be misled by it. A culture is not a doctrine or a set of consistent teachings or conclusions about a human life. It is not something we can set before ourselves as the subject of learning, any more than we can set self-understanding before ourselves as something to be learned; it is that which is learned in everything we may learn. A culture, particularly one such as ours, is a continuity of feelings, perceptions, ideas, engagements, attitudes and so forth, pulling in different directions, often critical of one another and contingently related to one another so as to compose not a doctrine, but what I shall call a conversational encounter. Ours, for example, accommodates not only the lyre of Apollo but also the pipes of Pan, the call of the wild; not only the poet but also the physicist; not only the majestic metropolis of Augustinian theology but also the 'greenwood' of Franciscan Christianity. A culture comprises unfinished intellectual and emotional journeyings, expeditions now abandoned but known to us in the tattered maps left behind by the explorers; it is composed of lighthearted adventures, of relationships invented and explored in exploit or in drama, of myths and stories and poems expressing fragments of human self-understanding, of gods worshipped, of responses to the mutability of the world and of encounters with death. And it reaches us, as it reached generations before ours, neither as long-ago terminated specimens of human adventure, nor as an accumulation of human achievements we are called upon to accept, but as a manifold of invitations to look, to listen and to reflect. Learning here is not merely acquiring information (*that* produces only what Nietzsche called a 'culture philistine'), nor is it merely 'improving one's mind'; it is learning to recognize some specific invitations to encounter particular adventures in human self-understanding.

A man's culture is an historic contingency, but since it is all he has he would be foolish to ignore it because it is not composed of eternal verities. It is itself a contingent flow of intellectual and emotional adventures, a mixture of old and new where the new is often a backward swerve to pick up what has been temporarily forgotten; a mixture of the emergent and the recessive; of the substantial and the somewhat flimsy, of the commonplace, the refined and the magnificent. Since learning is not, here, merely becoming aware of a so-called cultural inheritance but encountering and seeking to understand some of its specific invitations, a special place devoted to such learning is constituted only in terms of what it is believed there is to learn. Of course, this belief is itself a response to what may be called the 'educational' invitations of the culture. To talk of being 'culturally conditioned' is rubbish; a man is his culture, and what he is he has had to learn to become.

4

The wandering scholars who, in the twelfth century, took the road to Paris, to Bologna, to Chartres or to Toulouse were, often unknown to themselves, seeking within the notions of the time a 'liberal' education; they are our forebears in this adventure. You and I were born in the twelfth century and although we have travelled far we still bear the marks of our birth-time. But when two centuries later the expression 'liberal studies' acquired a specific meaning, it stood for an encounter with a somewhat remote culture which was slowly being retrieved from neglect – the Greek and Latin culture of antiquity. Some of the achievements of this ancient civilization had never been lost: the Latin language as a medium of communication, some useful information (mostly legal and medical) and some notable pieces of writing. But the educational adventure of the fourteenth century sprang from an ever more extended recovery of this almost lost culture which revealed itself not only to have been one of great intellectual splendour, variety and reflective energy but also to be one in which a man of the fourteenth century could identify himself and which offered him a wealth of hitherto unheard-of invitations to explore and to understand himself: languages recognized as investments in thought; epic, dramatic, lyric and historical literatures which gave a new dimension to human relationships, emotions, aspirations and conduct; enquiries (including those of the early theologians of Christianity) which suggested new directions for human reflection. Thus, 'learning' was identified with coming to understand the intimations of a human life displayed in an historic culture of remarkable splendour and lucidity and with the invitation to recognize oneself in terms of this culture. This was an education which promised and afforded liberation from the here and now of current engagements, from the muddle, the crudity, the sentimentality, the intellectual poverty and the emotional morass of ordinary life. And so it continues to this day. This education has had often to be rescued from the formalism into which it degenerated. Its centre of gravity moved from the culture of antiquity but without any firm settlement elsewhere. We have seen, sometimes regretfully, bits of this education fall away, having lost their compelling interest. It has been extended to include new and substantial vernacular languages and literatures. It has accommodated, somewhat reluctantly, the novel and still inadequately self-understood enquiry which has absorbed so much of the intellectual energy of modern times, namely the natural sciences. It has had to resist the seductive advances of enemies dressed up as friends. And what now of its present condition?

The engagement has survived. We do not yet live in the ashes of a great adventure which has burnt itself out. Its self-understanding is not at present very conspicuous, its self-confidence is fluctuating and often misplaced, its credit is stretched and it has borrowed when it would have been better to economize, but it has not been lacking in serious self-examination. The torch is still alight and there are still some hands to grasp it. But I shall not dwell upon its present vitality, such as it is; our concern is with its infirmities and with those that may be counted as self-betrayals – not to censure them but to try to understand them.

Its most naïve self-betrayal is merely to have listened to the seductive voice of the world urging it, in the name of 'relevance', to take up with extraneous concerns and even to alter course. When, like Ulysses, we should have stopped our ears with wax and bound ourselves to the mast of our own identity, we have been beguiled, not only by words but by inducements. To open a School of Business, to undertake the training of journalists or corporation lawyers seem harmless enough concessions to modernity; they may be defended by the specious argument that they certainly entail learning; they give a place of liberal learning an attractive image of 'relevance', and the corruption involved may be written off as negligible. Events, however, hardly confirm this optimism. Having no proper part in liberal learning, these appealing divergencies are difficult to contain; they undermine rather than assail the engagement. Their virtue is to be evanescent and contemporary; if they are not up-to-date they are worthless. And this unqualified modernity rubs off on the proper concern with languages, with literatures and with histories which are thus edged into the study of only what is current in a culture. History is contracted into what is called contemporary history, languages come to be recognized as means of contemporary communication, and in literature the book which 'verbalizes what everyone is thinking now' comes to be preferred, on that account, to anything else.

But the real assault upon liberal learning comes from another direction; not in the risky undertaking to equip learners for some, often prematurely chosen, profession, but in the belief that 'relevance' demands that every learner should be recognized as nothing but a role-performer is a so-called 'social system' and the consequent surrender of learning (which is the concern of individual persons) to 'socialization': the doctrine that because the current here and now is very much more uniform than it used to be, education should recognize and promote this uniformity. This is not a recent self-betrayal; it is the theme of those wonderful lectures of Nietzsche on the *Future of Our Educational Institutions* delivered in Basle a century ago in which he foresaw the collapse which now threatens us. And although this may seem to be very much a matter of doctrine, of merely how education is thought about and spoken of, and to have very little to do with what may actually go on in a place of learning, it is the most insidious of all corruptions. It not only strikes at the heart of liberal learning, it portends the abolition of man.

But if these are the cruder subversions of liberal learning there are others, more subtle but hardly less damaging. It has come to be thought of as a 'general' education; that is, as learning not only liberated from the here and now of current engagements but liberated also from an immediate concern with anything specific to be learned. Learning here is said to be 'learning to think for oneself' or to be the cultivation of 'intelligence' or of certain intellectual and moral aptitudes – the ability to 'think logically' or 'deliberatively', the ability not to be deceived by irrelevance in argument, to be courageous, patient, careful, accurate or determined; the ability to read attentively and to speak lucidly, and so on. And, of course, all these and more are aptitudes and virtues that a learner may hope to acquire or to improve. But neither they, nor self-understanding itself, can be made the subject of learning. A culture is not a set of abstract aptitudes; it is composed of substantive expressions of thought, emotion, belief, opinion, approval and disapproval, of moral and intellectual discriminations, of enquiries and investigations, and learning is coming to understand and respond to these substantive expressions of thought as invitations to think and to believe. Or, this word 'general' is used to identify and to recommend an education concerned, indeed, with the substance of a culture, but so anxious that everything shall receive mention that it can afford no more than a fleeting glimpse of anything in particular. Here learning amounts to little more than recognition; it never achieves the level of an encounter. It is the vague and fragmentary equipment of the 'culture philistine'.

Nevertheless, a place of liberal learning is rarely without a shape which purports to specify what there is to be learned. And its present shape in most such places bears witness both to the ancient lineage of the engagement and to the changes our culture has undergone in recent centuries. The natural sciences, mathematics, the humanities and the social sciences – these are the lineaments of this education as it comes to us now. Let us briefly consider these constituents.

Liberal learning is learning to respond to the invitations of the great intellectual adventures in which human beings have come to display their various understandings of the world and of themselves. The natural sciences, before they could be recognized in this character, had not only to offer something specific capable of

being learned but also to present themselves as a distinctive enquiry or mode of human understanding. That is to say, they had
to appear as very much more than somewhat mysterious information about the natural world which no educated man should
be without, and something very much less than an unconditional
or definitive understanding of the world. In respect of the first
they have amply succeeded: every natural science now presents
itself to the learner as a related set of theorems which invites
critical understanding. In respect of the second they have been
hindered, not by any inherent self-deception, but by two unfortunate circumstances. The first of these is the relic of a disposition
to value themselves in terms of the use which may be made of the
conclusions of their enquiries. This, in a place of liberal learning,
has sometimes led to a proliferation of what may be called semi-
sciences – organizations of information in terms of the use which
may be made of it. But this is not a very important hindrance. The
more serious encumbrance comes in some absurd claims made by
others on their behalf: the claim that they themselves compose a
distinctive culture (the silly doctrine of the 'two cultures'); the
claim that they represent 'the truth' (so far as it has been ascer-
tained) about the world; and the claim that they constitute the
model of all valid human understanding – a claim which has had
disastrous consequences elsewhere. But in spite of these hin-
drances, the natural sciences have unquestionably earned a proper
place for themselves in the design of liberal learning and know
how to occupy it. No doubt, for example, a biological identity is
not itself a human identity, but one of the significant self-understandings which human beings have come upon and explored is
that of persons concerned with a specifically 'scientific' understanding of themselves and the world.

Of the humanities I need say little. They are directly concerned
with expressions of human self-understanding and their place in
liberal learning is assured and central: languages recognized, not
as the means of contemporary communication but as investments
in thought and records of perceptions and analogical understandings; literatures recognized as the contemplative exploration of
beliefs, emotions, human characters and relationships in imagined
situations, liberated from the confused, cliché-ridden, generalized
conditions of commonplace life and constituting a world of ideal
human expressions inviting neither approval nor disapproval but
the exact attention and understanding of those who read; histories
recognized, not as accounts of the past focused upon our contemporary selves purporting to tell us how we have become what we

are and containing messages of warning or encouragement, but as stories in which human actions and utterances are rescued from mystery and made intelligible in terms of their contingent relationships; and philosophy, the reflective undertaking in which every purported achievement of human understanding becomes the subject of an enquiry into its conditions. If any of this has got driven off its course it is by the winds which forever blow around the engagement of liberal learning, menacing its seclusion from the here and now or driving it upon the rocks of abstract aptitudes or socialization.

But what of the latest-born component of liberal learning: the social sciences? They are a mixed lot. Among them we may expect to find sociology, anthropology, psychology, economics, perhaps jurisprudence and something called 'politics'. They purport to be directly conerned with human conduct. These are what used to be called the 'human sciences' – *Geisteswissenschaften* – in order to make clear that their concern is with human beings as self-conscious, intelligent persons who are what they understand themselves to be and not with human beings in the loose and indistinct sense of highly evolved organisms or processes of chemical change, the concern of natural sciences. And in so far as these human sciences are what they purport to be (which is not so in every case) it would seem that they belong properly to the 'humanities'. But distinguished they now are; and if the project of distinguishing them from the 'humanities' was an unfortunate mistake, the terms of the distinction are nothing less than a disaster. These terms are specified in the words 'social' and 'science'.

'Social', of course, is a cant word. It is used here to denote an enquiry about human conduct concerned not with substantive actions and utterances, but with the relationships, the associations and the practices in which human beings are joined. This focus of attention is not, in itself, corrupting. It is that upon which most histories of law are centred; and it is the focus, for example, of Maitland's *Constitutional History of England*, which, he tells us, is designed to be an account, not of human struggles, but of the results of human struggles in constitutional change. But it is chosen here, and is labelled 'social', in order to allege (or to suggest) that human beings and their performances are what they are in terms of these relationships, associations and practices; and to suggest, further, that these relationships and practices are not human devices, autonomous manners of being associated, each with its own specified conditions of relationship but are the components of an unspecified, unconditional interdependence or 'social' relationship,

something called a 'society' or 'Society'. In short, the contention is
that this unspecified 'social' relationship is the condition, perhaps
the determinant, of all human conduct and that to which human
actions and utterances must be referred in order to be understood.
To substitute the word 'social' for the word 'human' is to surrender
to confusion: human conduct is never merely a subscription to a
practice or to a relationship, and there is no such thing as an unconditional 'social' relationship. This confusion is partnered by
a commonplace corruption of our language in which the word
'social' has become the centre of endless equivocation. John Selden
in the seventeenth century said of the cant expression *scrutamini
scripturas*, 'these two words have undone the world'; a single word
has sufficed to undo our cruder twentieth century.

It might, however, be supposed that in connecting the word
'science' with the word 'social' something has been done to restore
exactness. But the outcome of this conjunction has been to add a
ruinous categorical confusion to what need not have been more
than a permissible partiality in considering human conduct. For
the word 'science' in this context is intended to denote a natural
science of human conduct; that is, to mean the investigation of
human actions and utterances and the practices and relationships
to which they may subscribe as if they were non-intelligent components of a 'process', or the functional constituents of a 'system',
which do not have to learn their parts in order to play them.
The design here is to remove human action and utterance from
the category of intelligent goings-on (that is, chosen responses of
self-conscious agents to their understood situations which have
reasons but not causes and may be understood only in terms of
dispositions, beliefs, meanings, intentions and motives); to place
them in the category of examples of the operation of regularities
which do not have to be learned in order to be observed; and to
remove human practices, relationships, associations and so forth
from the category of procedures whose conditions have to be
learned and understood in order to be subscribed to and can be
subscribed to only in self-chosen actions and utterances, and to put
them into the category of 'processes'. Rules are misidentified as
regularities, intelligent winks as physiological blinks, conduct as
'behaviour' and contingent relationships as causal or systematic
connections.

This project of collecting together a number of respectable enquiries under the head of 'the social sciences' and the attempt to
impose this equivocal character upon them has not met with universal acceptance but it has gone far enough to have deeply dam-

aged liberal learning; no other failure of self-understanding in the humanities has generated such confusion. It is all the more damaging because, in putting on the mask of 'science', some of these departments of learning have succumbed to the temptation to understand and to value themselves in terms of the use that may be made of the conclusions of their enquiries. Their recognition as the appropriate equipment for new technological enterprises and for the new and proliferating profession of 'social worker' has corrupted liberal learning. But this does not mean that, individually, and when properly recognized as *Geisteswissenschaften*, they have no proper place in liberal learning; it means only that they have been misidentified. Jurisprudence, until it was confused with a vapid concern for so-called social and psychological needs and became part of the equipment of 'social engineers', was a profound philosophical enquiry, one of the most ancient and respected components of liberal learning. Sociology and anthropology are respectable and somewhat attenuated engagements in historical understanding; they are concerned with human practices, procedures, associations and so forth, and their contingent relations, and with human actions and utterances in terms of their subscriptions to the conditions of practices. Psychology has long ago declared itself a 'natural', not a 'human', science. It is not concerned with substantive human thoughts, beliefs, emotions, recollections, actions and utterances but with so-called 'mental processes' which are vulnerable to reduction to genetic and chemical processes.

5

Putting on one side engagements in learning that have no proper place in a liberal education, there are, then, departments of liberal learning in which self-consciousness has not yet been transformed into the self-understanding upon which authentic enquiry and utterance depends. But the more serious consideration for anyone who undertakes to review the present condition of liberal learning is the terms of the self-understanding of the engagement itself.

As it emerged in Western Europe, liberal learning was understood to be a concern to explore the invitations of the culture of antiquity, to hold before learners the mirror of this culture so that, seeing themselves reflected in it, they might extend the range and the depth of their understanding of themselves. This idiom of the self-understanding of liberal learning was never very satisfactory; it was substantial, not formal, and it has long since passed away.

It has been succeeded by other, similarly substantial, self-identifi-
cations. For example, when I was young it was thought (or at least
suggested) that the whole of liberal learning might properly be
understood in terms of a somewhat extended study of Geography:
liberal learning was urged to find the focus of its attention in
'geographical man'. And we have since become familiar with a
claim of this sort made on behalf of Sociology; if every department
of liberal learning is not itself to be turned into sociology (philosophy into the sociology of knowledge, jurisprudence into the
sociology of law and so forth) then, at least, none is as it should be
unless sociology were added to it. These, of course, are fanciful
notions, but they are not unconvincing merely on account of their
contingent implausibility. They are unacceptable because the
identification of liberal learning they suggest is of the wrong kind.
The self-understanding of liberal learning must, I think, be sought
in the recognition that its component enquiries, in spite of their
substantial differences, have a common formal character and that
they are related to one another in a manner agreeable with that
formal character.

I have already suggested that the components of a liberal education are united and distinguished from what does not properly
belong to it in terms of their 'liberality'; that is, in terms of their
concern with what Valéry calls *le prix de la vie humaine*,[3] and their
emancipation from the here and now of current engagements.
But beyond this general consideration, these components may be
resolved into and understood as so many different languages: the
language of the natural sciences, for example, the language of
history, the language of philosophy, or the language of poetic
imagination.

Languages in a more commonplace sense are organizations of
grammatical and syntactical considerations or rules to be taken
account of and subscribed to in making utterances. These considerations do not determine the utterances made or even exactly
how they shall be subscribed to; that is left to the speaker who
not only has something of his own to say but may also have a
style of his own. Of course, no such language is ever settled beyond
the reach of modification; to speak it is a linguistically inventive
engagement. The conditions imposed upon utterance by these languages of understanding constitute not merely linguistic idioms,
but particular conditional modes of understanding. Learning here
is learning to recognize and discriminate between these languages

---

[3] 'Tout ce qui fait le prix de la vie est curieusement inutile.'

of understanding, is becoming familiar with the conditions each imposes upon utterance, and is learning to make utterances whose virtue is not that they express original ideas (that can only be a rare achievement) but that they display genuine understanding of the language spoken. It is on this account that a learner may be recognized to understand a language such as that of philosophical or historical understanding and yet not be a philosopher or an historian; and also that a teacher may be recognized to have something into which he may initiate a learner which is not itself a doctrine. But since none of these languages of understanding was invented yesterday and each is the continuous exploration of its own possibilities, a learner cannot expect to find what he seeks if he attends only to contemporary utterances. These languages of understanding like other languages are known only in literatures.

What I am suggesting, then, is that from the standpoint of liberal learning, a culture is not a miscellany of beliefs, perceptions, ideas, sentiments and engagements, but may be recognized as a variety of distinct languages of understanding, and its inducements are invitations to become acquainted with these languages, to learn to discriminate between them, and to recognize them not merely as diverse modes of understanding the world but as the most substantial expressions we have of human self-understanding.

Yet the identity of a culture and of liberal learning remains obscure until we have some conception of the relationship of its components. Now each of these languages constitutes the terms of a distinct, conditional understanding of the world and a similarly distinct idiom of human self-understanding. Their virtue is to be different from one another and this difference is intrinsic. Each is secure in its autonomy so long as it knows and remains faithful to itself. Any of them may fail, but such failure is always self-defeat arising from imperfect understanding of itself or from the non-observance of its own conditions. They may not all be equally interesting and they may compete for our attention, but they are not inherently contentious and they are incapable of refuting one another. Hence, their relationship cannot be that of parties in a debate; they do not together compose an argument. Further, they are not differing degrees of divergence from some suppositious unconditional understanding of the world: their relationship is not hierarchical. Nor is it either a co-operative or a transactional relationship. They are not partners in a common undertaking, each with a role to perform, nor are they suppliers of one another's wants. What then is left?

Perhaps we may think of these components of a culture as voices, each the expression of a distinct and conditional understanding of the world and a distinct idiom of human self-understanding, and of the culture itself as these voices joined, as such voices could only be joined, in a conversation – an endless unrehearsed intellectual adventure in which, in imagination, we enter into a variety of modes of understanding the world and ourselves and are not disconcerted by the differences or dismayed by the inconclusiveness of it all. And perhaps we may recognize liberal learning as, above all else, an education in imagination, an initiation into the art of this conversation in which we learn to recognize the voices; to distinguish their different modes of utterance, to acquire the intellectual and moral habits appropriate to this conversational relationship and thus to make our *début dans la vie humaine*.

6

Liberal learning is a difficult engagement. It depends upon an understanding of itself which is always imperfect; even those who presided over its emergence hardly knew what they were doing. And it depends upon a self-confidence which is easily shaken and not least by continual self-examination. It is a somewhat unexpected invitation to disentangle oneself from the here and now of current happenings and engagements, to detach oneself from the urgencies of the local and the contemporary, to explore and enjoy a release from having to consider things in terms of their contingent features, beliefs in terms of their applications to contingent situations and persons in terms of their contingent usefulness; an invitation to be concerned not with the employment of what is familiar but with understanding what is not yet understood. A university as a place of liberal learning can prosper only if those who come are disposed to recognize and acknowledge its particular invitation to learn. Its present predicament lies in the circumstance that there is now so much to obstruct this disposition.

There was a time, not so long ago, when liberal learning was, not better understood, but more generally recognized than it now is and when the obtrusive circumstances of the early upbringing of many (and not merely of the better off) were such that they did not positively stand in the way of the recognition of its invitation. They were, indeed, circumstances where the localities in which one was born and grew up were more enclosed than they now are and certainly less superficially exciting. Memorable experiences were fewer and smaller, there was change but it moved at a slower pace; life could be hard but the rat race as we know it now was in its infancy. They were also somewhat narrow circumstances which bred little concern with what might be going on outside the locality and none at all with world affairs. But they were intellectually innocent rather than positively dull, uncrowded rather than vacant. For there was in these circumstances a notable absence of the ready-made or of oppressive uniformities of thought or attitude or conduct. If experiences were fewer, they were made to go further; if they were smaller, they invoked imaginative enlargement. The natural world was never so far distant as it now often is and the response to it was allowed to be naïve and uncluttered, a response of wonder and delight. In all this, School was important; but it was a place of its own. I often recollect that memorable sentence from the autobiography of Sir Ernest Barker: 'Outside the cottage, I had nothing but my school; but having my school I had everything'. There, in school, the narrow boundaries of the local and the contemporary were swept aside to reveal, not what might be going on in the next town or village, in Parliament or in the United Nations, but a world of things and persons and happenings, of languages and beliefs, of utterances and sights and sounds past all imagination and to which even the dullest could not be wholly indifferent. The going was hard; there was nothing to be got without learning how to get it, and it was understood that nobody went to school in order to enjoy the sort of happiness he might get from lying in the sun. And when with inky fingers a schoolboy unpacked his satchel to do his homework he unpacked three thousand years of the fortunes and misfortunes of human intellectual adventure. Nor would it easily have occurred to him to ask what the sufferings of Job, the silent ships moving out of Tenedos in the moonlight, the terror, the complication and the pity of the human condition revealed in a drama of Shakespeare or Racine, or even the chemical composition of water, had to do with *him*, born upon the banks of the Wabash, in the hills of Cumberland, in a Dresden suburb or a Neapolitan slum. Either he never considered the question at all, or he dimly recognized them as images of a human self-understanding which was to be his for the learning. All very innocent, perhaps even credulous; and in many cases soon overlaid by the urgencies of current engagements. But however superficially they might be appreciated, these were not circumstances which generated a positive resistance to the invitation of liberal learning in a university. Indeed, their very innocence nurtured a disposition to recognize it.

But these circumstances are no longer with us. The way we live now, even though it may contain notable relics of the earlier condition, is somewhat different. The world in which many children now grow up is crowded, not necessarily with occupants and not at all with memorable experiences, but with happenings; it is a ceaseless flow of seductive trivialities which invoke neither reflection nor choice but instant participation. A child quickly becomes aware that he cannot too soon plunge into this flow or immerse himself in it too quickly; to pause is to be swept with the chilling fear of never having lived at all. There is little chance that his perceptions, his emotions, his admirations and his ready indignations might become learned responses or be even innocent fancies of his own; they come to him prefabricated, generalized and uniform. He lurches from one modish conformity to the next, or from one fashionable guru to his successor, seeking to lose himself in a solidarity composed of exact replicas of himself. From an early age children now believe themselves to be well-informed about the world, but they know it only at second-hand in the pictures and voices that surround them. It holds no puzzles or mysteries for them; it invites neither careful attention nor understanding. As like as not they know the moon as something to be shot at or occupied before ever they have had the chance to marvel at it. This world has but one language, soon learned: the language of appetite. The idiom may be that of the exploitation of the resources of the earth, or it may be that of seeking something for nothing; but this is distinction without a difference. It is a language composed of meaningless clichés. It allows only the expression of 'points of view' and the ceaseless repetition of slogans which are embraced as prophetic utterances. Their ears are filled with the babel of invitations to instant and unspecified reactions and their utterance reproduces only what they have heard said. Such discourse as there is resembles the barking of a dog at the echo of its own yelp. School in these circumstances is notably unimportant. To a large extent it has surrendered its character as a place apart where utterances of another sort may be heard and languages other than the language of appetite may be learned. It affords no seclusion, it offers no release. Its furnishings are the toys with which those who come are already familiar. Its virtues and its vices are those of the surrounding world.

These, then, are circumstances hostile to a disposition to recognize the invitation of liberal learning; that is, the invitation to disentangle oneself, for a time, from the urgencies of the here and now and to listen to the conversation in which human beings forever seek to understand themselves. How shall a university respond to the current aversion from seclusion, to the now common belief that there are other and better ways of becoming human than by learning to do so, and to the impulsive longing to be given a doctrine or to be socialized according to a formula rather than to be initiated into a conversation? Not, I think, by seeking excuses for what sometimes seem unavoidable surrenders, nor in any grand gesture of defiance, but in a quiet refusal to compromise which comes only in self-understanding. We must remember who we are: inhabitants of a place of liberal learning.

LEARNING AND TEACHING

1965

Learning is the comprehensive engagement in which we come to know ourselves and the world around us. It is a paradoxical activity: it is doing and submitting at the same time. And its achievements range from merely being aware, to what may be called understanding and being able to explain.

In each of us, it begins at birth; it takes place not in some ideal abstract world, but in the local world we inhabit; for the individual it terminates only in death, for a civilization it ends in the collapse of the characteristic manner of life, and for the race it is, in principle, interminable.

The activity of learning may, however, be suspended from time to time while we enjoy what we have learned. The distinction between a driver and a learner-driver is not insignificant; a master-tailor making a suit of clothes is doing something other than learning to make a suit of clothes. But the suspension is, perhaps, never either decisive or complete: learning itself often entails practising what we have in some sense learned already, and there is probably a component of learning in every notable performance. Moreover, some activities, like intellectual enquiries, remain always activities of learning.

By learning I mean an activity possible only to an intelligence capable of choice and self-direction in relation to his own impulses and to the world around him. These, of course, are pre-eminently human characteristics, and, as I understand it, only human beings are capable of learning. A learner is not a passive recipient of

43

impressions, nor one whose accomplishments spring from mere reactions to circumstances, nor one who attempts nothing he does not know how to accomplish. He is a creature of wants rather than of needs, of recollection as well as memory; he wants to know what to think and what to believe and not merely what to do. Learning concerns conduct, not behaviour. In short, these analogies of clay and wax, of receptacles to be filled and empty rooms to be furnished, have nothing to do with learning and learners.

I do not mean that the attention of a learner is focused always upon understanding and being able to explain, or that nothing can be learned which is not understood; nor do I mean that human beings are uniquely predestined learners whatever their circumstances. I mean only that an activity which may include understanding and being able to explain within its range is different, not only at this point, but at all points in the scale of its achievements, from one to which this possibility is denied.

Teaching is a practical activity in which a 'learned' person (to use an archaism) 'learns' his pupils. No doubt one may properly be said to learn from books, from gazing at the sky or from listening to the waves (so long as one's disposition is that mixture of activity and submission we call curiosity), but to say that the book, the sky or the sea has taught us anything, or that we have taught ourselves, is to speak in the language of unfortunate metaphor. The counterpart of the teacher is not the learner in general, but the pupil. And I am concerned with the learner as pupil, one who learns from a teacher, one who learns by being taught. This does not mean that I subscribe to the prejudice that attributes all learning to teaching; it means only that I am concerned here with learning when it is the counterpart of teaching.

The activity of the teacher is, then, specified in the first place by the character of his partner. The ruler is partnered by the citizen, the physician by his patient, the master by his servant, the duenna by her charge, the commander by his subordinates, the lawyer by his client, the prophet by his disciple, the clown by his audience, the hypnotist by his subject, and both the tamer and trainer by creatures whose aptitudes are those of being tamed or trained. Each of these is engaged in a practical activity, but it is not teaching; each has a partner, but he is not a pupil. Teaching is not taming, ruling, restoring to health, conditioning, or commanding, because none of these activities is possible in relation to a pupil. Like the ruler, or the hypnotist, the teacher communicates something to his partner; his peculiarity is that what he communicates is appropriate to a partner who is a pupil – it is something which may be received only by being learned. And there can, I think, be no doubt about what this is.

Every human being is born an heir to an inheritance to which he can succeed only in a process of learning. If this inheritance were an estate composed of woods and meadows, a villa in Venice, a portion of Pimlico and a chain of village stores, the heir would expect to succeed to it automatically, on the death of his father or on coming of age. It would be conveyed to him by lawyers, and the most that would be expected of him would be legal acknowledgement.

But the inheritance I speak of is not exactly like this; and, indeed, this is not exactly as I have made it out to be. What every man is born an heir to is an inheritance of human achievements; an inheritance of feelings, emotions, images, visions, thoughts, beliefs, ideas, understandings, intellectual and practical enterprises, languages, relationships, organizations, canons and maxims of conduct, procedures, rituals, skills, works of art, books, musical compositions, tools, artefacts and utensils – in short, what Dilthey called a *geistige Welt*.

The components of this world are not abstractions ('physical objects') but beliefs. It is a world of facts, not 'things'; of 'expressions' which have meanings and require to be understood because they are the 'expressions' of human minds. The landed estate itself belongs to this world; indeed, this is the only world known to human beings. The starry heavens above us and the moral law within are alike human achievements. And it is a world, not because it has itself any meaning (it has none), but because it is a whole of interlocking meanings which establish and interpret one another.

This world can be entered, possessed and enjoyed only in a process of learning. A 'picture' may be purchased, but one cannot purchase an understanding of it. And I have called this world our common inheritance because to enter it is the only way of becoming a human being, and to inhabit it is to be a human being. It is into this *geistige Welt* that the child, even in its earliest adventures in awareness, initiates itself; and to initiate his pupils into it is the business of the teacher. Not only may it be entered only by learning, but there is nothing else for a pupil to learn. If, from one point of view, the analogies of wax and clay are inappropriate to learning, from another point of view the analogies of sagacious apes and accomplished horses are no less inappropriate. These admirable creatures have no such inheritance; they may only be trained to react to a stimulus and to perform tricks.[1]

There is an ancient oriental image of human life which recognizes this account of our circumstances. In it the child is understood to owe its physical life to its father, a debt to be acknowledged with appropriate respect. But initiation into the *geistige Welt* of human achievement is owed to the Sage, the teacher: and this debt is to be acknowledged with the profoundest reverence – for to whom can a man be more deeply indebted than to the one to whom he owes, not his mere existence, but his participation in human life? It is the Sage, the teacher, who is the agent of civilization. And, as Dr. Johnson said, not to name the school and the masters of illustrious men is a kind of historical fraud.

2

Most of what I have to say about learning and teaching relates to the character of what is taught and learned, and to the bearing of this upon the activities concerned; but there are two general considerations, one about the teacher and the other about the pupil, which I must notice first.

It is difficult to think of any circumstances where learning may be said to be impossible. Of course, in some conditions it will take place more rapidly and more successfully than in others; but, in principle, it does not depend upon any specifiable degree of attention, and it is not uncommon to find oneself to have learned without knowing how or when it happened. Thus, the random utterances of anyone, however foolish or ignorant, may serve to enlighten a learner, who receives from them as much or as little as he happens to be ready to receive, and receives often what the speaker did not himself know or did not know he was conveying.

But such casual utterances are not teaching; and he who scatters them is not, properly speaking, a teacher. Teaching is the deliberate and intentional initiation of a pupil into the world of human achievement, or into some part of it. The teacher is one whose

[1] The horses I refer to are, of course, those of Elberfield. But it is, perhaps, worth recalling that the ancient Athenians delighted in the horse above all other animals because they recognized in it an affinity to man, and an animal uniquely capable of education. The horse had no *geistige* inheritance of its own, but (while other animals might be set to work) the horse was capable of sharing an inheritance imparted to it by man. And, in partnership with a rider (so Xenophon observed), it could acquire talents, accomplishments and even a grace of movement unknown to it in its 'natural' condition.

utterances (or silences) are designed to promote this initiation in respect of a pupil – that is, in respect of a learner whom he recognizes to be ready to receive what he has resolved to communicate. In short, a pupil is a learner known to a teacher; and teaching, properly speaking, is impossible in his absence.

This, of course, does not mean that 'readiness to receive' is an easily discernible condition, or that it should be identified as the condition in which reception will come most easily. Jean Paul Richter's maxim, that in teaching a two-year-old one should speak to him as if he were six, may be a profound observation. Nor does it mean that the relationship of teacher and pupil is emancipated from the latitudes and imprecisions common to all human relationships. Indeed, it is probably more subject to these imprecisions than any other relationship. What it means is that a teacher is one who studies his pupil, that the initiation *he* undertakes is one which has a deliberate order and arrangement, and that, as well as knowing what he designs to transmit, he has considered the manner of transmission. I once knew a wise man who, wishing to learn the art of the farrier, looked, not only for a man practised in the art, but for one accustomed to teaching, and he was gratified when he found a farrier who was also a teacher of boxing.

With regard to the pupil, there is a famous dilemma which has haunted reflection on education for long enough. Is learning to be understood as acquiring knowledge, or is it to be regarded as the development of the personality of the learner? Is teaching concerned with initiating a pupil into an inheritance of human achievement, or is it enabling the pupil to make the most or the best of himself? Like many such cruxes, this one points to what I believe to be a genuine discrepancy, but misinterprets it.

To escape from it we may recognize learning, not merely as the acquisition of knowledge, but also as the extension of the ability to learn, as the education and not merely the furnishing of a mind, as an inheritance coming to be possessed in such a manner that it loses its second-hand or antique character; and we may recognize teaching, not as passing on something to be received, nor as merely planting a seed, but as setting on foot the cultivation of a mind so that what is planted may grow. But the escape from the dilemma this affords us is imperfect; and, in any case, it is not an escape but a resolution we should be seeking.

What, I think, we must understand is that there is no discrepancy between a pupil succeeding to his inheritance of human achievement and his making the most of himself. 'Self-realization' for human beings is not, of course, the realization of an exactly predetermined end which requires only circumstances favourable to this end in order that it should be achieved; but nor is this self an infinite, unknown potentiality which an inheritance of human achievement is as likely to thwart as to promote. Selves are not rational abstractions, they are historic personalities, they are among the components of this world of human achievements; and there is no other way for a human being to make the most of himself than by learning to recognize himself in the mirror of this inheritance.

A discrepancy, however, remains; but it is a discrepancy, not between the self and its world, but between learning and teaching. It is a divergence of points of view. For the pupil, to learn is not to endeavour to make the most of himself, it is to acquire knowledge, to distinguish between truth and error, to understand and become possessor of what he was born heir to. But to the teacher things must appear differently. Obliquely and upon a consequence he is an agent of civilization. But his direct relationship is with his pupil. His engagement is, specifically, to get his pupil to make the most of himself by teaching him to recognize himself in the mirror of the human achievements which compose his inheritance. This is the somewhat complicated manner in which he performs his work of initiation, and this is what distinguishes him from others who hand on the fruits of civilization; namely, that he has a pupil.

Now, to make a 'civilization' available to a pupil is not to put him in touch with the dead, nor is it to rehearse before him the social history of mankind. Death belongs to nature, not *Geist*; and it is only in nature that generation involves a process of recapitulating all earlier forms of life. To initiate a pupil into the world of human achievement is to make available to him much that does not lie upon the surface of his present world. An inheritance will contain much that may not be in current use, much that has come to be neglected and even something that for the time being is forgotten. And to know only the dominant is to become acquainted with only an attenuated version of this inheritance. To see oneself reflected in the mirror of the present modish world is to see a sadly distorted image of a human being; for there is nothing to encourage us to believe that what has captured current fancy is the most valuable part of our inheritance, or that the better survives more readily than the worse. And nothing survives in this world which is not cared for by human beings. The business of the teacher (indeed, this may be said to be his peculiar quality as an agent of civilization) is to release his pupils from servitude to the current dominant feelings, emotions, images, ideas, beliefs and even skills, not by inventing alternatives to them which seem to him more desirable, but by making available to him something which approximates more closely to the whole of his inheritance.

But this inheritance is an historic achievement; it is 'positive', not 'necessary'; it is contingent upon circumstances; it is miscellaneous and incoherent; it is what human beings have achieved, not by the impulsion of a final cause, but by exploiting the opportunities of fortune and by means of their own efforts. It comprises the standards of conduct to which from time to time they have given their preferences, the pro and con feelings to which they have given their approval and disapproval, the intellectual enterprises they have happened upon and pursued, the duties they have imposed upon themselves, the activities they have delighted in, the hopes they have entertained and the disappointments they have suffered. The notions of 'finished' and 'unfinished' are equally inapplicable to it. It does not deliver to us a clear and unambiguous message; it often speaks in riddles; it offers us advice and suggestion, recommendations, aids to reflection, rather than directives. It has been put together not by designers but by men who knew only dimly what they did. It has no meaning as a whole; it cannot be learned or taught in principle, only in detail.

A teacher, then, engaged in initiating his pupils into so contingent an inheritance, might be excused for thinking that he needed some assurance of its worth. For, like many of us, he may be expected to have a superstitious prejudice against the human race and to be satisfied only when he can feel himself anchored to something for which human beings are not responsible. But he must be urged to have the courage of his circumstances. This man-made inheritance contains everything to which value may be attributed; it is the ground and context of every judgement of better and worse. If there were a mirror of perfection which he could hold up to his pupils, he might be expected to prefer it to this home-made article. But there is no such mirror. He may be excused if he finds the present dominant image of civilized life too disagreeable to impart with any enthusiasm to his pupils. But if he has no confidence in any of the standards of worth written into this inheritance of human achievement, he had better not be a teacher; he would have nothing to teach.

But teachers are modest people, and we are likely to disclaim so large an engagement as initiating our pupils into the civilized inheritance of mankind. We do not pretend to hand on anything but scraps of that inheritance; and it does not escape us that the civilization we are directly concerned with is not alone in the world and that this is a further limitation of our activities. And all this constitutes a renewed recognition of the contingency of what we have to teach. But the important point here is that whether we are concerned with a relatively simple or (like ours) an exceedingly complex civilization, whether we are concerned with a small or a large part of it, and whether we are concerned with practical skills, with moral conduct or with large intellectual enterprises (like philosophy or science), teaching and learning always relate to an historic inheritance of human achievement and that what is to be handed on and learned, known and understood, are thoughts and various 'expressions' of thoughts.

3

From one important point of view, all we can be said to know constitutes a manifold of different 'abilities', different amounts of knowledge being represented in different degrees of ability, and every complex ability being a manifold of simpler abilities.

When an ability is recognized as an ability to do or to make something, and it is recognized to be significantly composed of physical movements, we usually call it a skill. Playing billiards and ploughing a field are skills; each may be enjoyed in different degrees and each may be seen to be a manifold of simpler skills. Thus the ability to plough entails the ability to manage the horse as well as the plough; and the ability to manage the horse entails the ability to manage the leads and the ability to make the appropriate noises.

Further, we are apt to extend this notion of skill to abilities not so significantly composed of physical movements. A navigator, a chairman or a painter may be said to be 'skilful'. But when we say this we usually mean that the abilities concerned in these activities are large and complex and that in this case they are enjoyed only to a limited extent: we mean that his ability runs to a *merely* skilful performance. And this draws attention to abilities which we do not normally call skills.

These are usually more complicated, less obviously concerned with doing and making and more obviously concerned with the performance of mental operations – like speaking, diagnosing, understanding, describing, explaining, etc. The complex 'abilities' denoted in the expressions engineer, Latin scholar, explorer, actor, surgeon, lawyer, army commander, physicist, teacher, painter, farmer and so forth are each manifolds in which simpler abilities are grouped and given a specific focus.

This conjunction, in a concept of 'abilities', of what we know and the use we make of it, is not designed to prove anything, but merely to indicate the way in which we carry about with us what we may be said to know. What we are aware of is not a number of items of knowledge available for use, but having powers of specific kinds – the power of being able to solve a legal problem, or to understand a Latin inscription or to perform a surgical operation. What we know constitutes an equipment which we possess in terms of what it enables us to do or to understand. The 'pragmatism' which this way of thinking might seem to commit us to may be avoided if it is recognized that abilities are of different kinds and cannot be assimilated to one another – that, for example, the ability to understand and to explain cannot be assimilated to the ability to do or to make.

Now, these abilities of various kinds and dimensions which constitute what we may be said to know will be found to be conjunctions of what is called 'information' and what I shall call 'judgement'.

The component of 'information' is easily recognized. It is the explicit ingredient of knowledge, where what we know may be itemized. Information consists of facts, specific intellectual artefacts (often arranged in sets or bunches). It is impersonal (not a matter of opinion). Most of it is accepted on authority, and it is to be found in dictionaries, manuals, textbooks and encyclopaedias. It is the appropriate answer to questions which ask: who? what? where? which? how long? how much? etc. Typical pieces of information are: the date of Shakespeare's death or St. Paul's conversion; the average annual rainfall in Bournemouth; the ingredients of Welsh rabbit; the specific gravity of alcohol; the age of consent; the atomic structure of nitrogen; the reasons given by Milton for favouring polygamy; the seating capacity of the Albert Hall.

Except in quizzes, where it is notoriously inert, information is a component of knowledge, and (unlike knowledge itself) it may be useful or useless. Useful information is composed of facts related to a particular skill or ability. There is no inherently useless information; there are only facts irrelevant to the matter in hand.

Some facts seem to convey detached pieces of information – 'Mummy, Mrs. Smith wears a wig', 'we cook on gas', 'that is a bicycle', 'this is a bassoon' – and they lose their inertness merely by reason of their place in a conversation. But the importance of information lies in its provision of rules or rule-like propositions relating to abilities. Every ability has its rules, and they are contained in that component of knowledge we call information. This is clearly the case with mathematical or chemical formulae, or with information like 'glass is brittle' or 'hemlock is poisonous'; but it is also the case with other items of information. A recipe tells me what ingredients I should use in making a dish, and one of the uses of knowing the seating capacity of the Albert Hall is that it tells me how many tickets I may sell.

But rules or rule-like propositions such as are supplied in pieces of information may be related to knowledge (that is, to a specific ability or skill) in either of two different ways. They may be items of information which must be known as a condition of being able to perform; or they may constitute the criterion by means of which a performance may be known to be incorrect, though here they are never the only means by which mistakes may be detected.

First, nobody could read or receive a message in Morse unless he were correctly informed about the Morse Code equivalents of the letters of the alphabet. This is information in the exact sense. It is a set of facts (specific intellectual artefacts), not opinions; it is stated in propositions; it is received on authority; it is capable of being forgotten and it needs to be recollected; and it appears in rules to be followed – rules which must be known and recollected as a condition of being able to perform.

Secondly, the grammar of a language may be said to constitute the criterion by which a performance may be known to be incorrect. It consists of facts, stated in propositions, and it appears as rules. But, while this information may obliquely promote a laudable performance, it is not necessary to it. A laudable performance is possible to somebody who never possessed this information, or to somebody who once had it but has now forgotten it. There are a number of things directly related to a performance which a person ignorant of these facts could not do; but among them is neither the ability to speak intelligently and to understand what is said in the language, nor the ability to detect mistakes. The rules, here, are observed in the performance and they are capable of being known. They are the criteria for determining an incorrect performance, but a knowledge of them is not a condition of a laudable performance.

There is, indeed, a third sort of rule-like proposition which, in order to distinguish it from other sorts, is often called a 'principle'. These are propositions which are advanced in order to explain what is going on in any performance; they supply what may be called its 'underlying rationale'. And, consequently, as I understand them, they are never components of the knowledge which constitutes the performance. They belong to a separate performance of their own – the performance of explaining a performance. Let me offer two examples of what I mean.

First, riding a bicycle is a skill which consists wholly of making the appropriate physical movements. In order to enjoy this skill certain information must have been acquired, and there may also be what could be called the 'grammar' of the skill. But beyond all this, the skill may be said to be an exemplification of certain principles of mechanics. But these principles are utterly unknown to even the most successful cyclist, and being able to recite them would not help him to be more proficient. They do not constitute a criterion. Their sole value is the contribution they may make to our understanding of what is going on. In short, they are unrelated either to learning or to practising the skill. They belong to a separate performance, the performance of explaining.

Secondly, moral conduct may be said to be the ability to behave well. Here, again, certain information must be known; and there may also be what could be called the 'grammar' of moral conduct – the rules and rule-like propositions which constitute the criteria by means of which a performance may be known to be 'incorrect'. But, again, beyond all this there are, or may be, 'principles' in terms of which what is going on in moral conduct may be understood and explained. Aristotle, for example, in the 'principle of the Mean', formulated what he believed to be the 'underlying rationale' of all good conduct. But a knowledge of this, or of any other such 'principle', is not a condition of being able to behave well, nor does this principle constitute a criterion by means of which a performance may be known to be 'incorrect'. It is unrelated either to learning good conduct or to a good performance.

There is, then, as I understand it, a sort of information which is designed to explain a performance (and also to explain the rules of a performance), but which is never a component of the knowledge which constitutes the performance. This, of course, is so even when the performance is itself a performance of understanding and explanation, as, for example, in history or in science.

But, to return from this not unnecessary digression, there is in all knowledge an ingredient of information. It consists of facts which may range from the recognitions and identifications in which knowledge of any sort emerges from indeterminate awareness, to rules or rule-like propositions which inform the skills and abilities in which we carry about what we may be said to know, and which are sometimes, but not always, expressly known and followed. This ingredient of information, however, never constitutes the whole of what we know. Before any concrete skill or ability can appear, information must be partnered by 'judgement', 'knowing *how*' must be added to the 'knowing *what*' of information.

By 'judgement' I mean the tacit or implicit component of knowl-

edge, the ingredient which is not merely unspecified in propositions but is unspecifiable in propositions. It is the component of
knowledge which does not appear in the form of rules and which,
therefore, cannot be resolved into information or itemized in the
manner characteristic of information.

That we enjoy such knowledge has seemed to some writers undeniable. They direct our attention, in the first place, to skills –
that is, to abilities which are significantly composed of physical
movements. We may know how to do something without being
able to state explicitly the manner of acting involved. This, for
example, appears to be the case in swimming, riding a horse, playing a fish, using a chisel and in turning a bowl on a potter's wheel.
These writers point out, further, that we may recognize an action
as being of a known kind without being able to specify how we
recognized it; that we are able to discover similarities in things
without being able to say what they consist of, or patterns without
being aware of the elements they are composed of or the rules they
exemplify; and that we may speak a language without knowing the
rules we are following and even without those rules ever having
been formulated.

All this, I think, is true. But what it suggests to me is that there
are skills and abilities where what is known may lack certain sorts
of informatory content (particularly the sort of information we call
'the rules'), rather than that there is a 'knowing *how*' which can be
divorced from any 'knowing *what*'. Thus I have used 'judgement'
to distinguish 'knowing *how*' from information because I think
'knowing *how*' is an ingredient of all genuine knowledge, and not a
separate kind of knowing specified by an ignorance of rules.

Facts, rules, all that may come to us as information, itemized
and explicit, never themselves endow us with an ability to do, or to
make, or to understand and explain anything. Information has to
be used, and it does not itself indicate how, on any occasion, it
should be used. What is required in addition to information is
knowledge which enables us to interpret it, to decide upon its
relevance, to recognize what rule to apply and to discover what
action permitted by the rule should, in the circumstances, be performed; knowledge (in short) capable of carrying us across those
wide open spaces, to be found in every ability, where no rule runs.
For rules are always disjunctive. They specify only an act or a conclusion of a certain general kind and they never relieve us of the
necessity of choice. They never yield more than partial explanations: to understand anything as an example of the operation of a
rule is to understand it very imperfectly.

'Judgement', then, is not to be recognized as merely information of another sort; its deliverances cannot be itemized, remembered or forgotten. It is, for example, all that is contained in what has been called 'the unspecifiable art of scientific enquiry' without which 'the articulate contents of scientific knowledge' remains unintelligible.

And if we are obliged to retreat a little from the notion of an entirely independent 'knowing *how*' (because every ability has an ingredient of fact, recognized as fact and specifiable in propositions), I do not think we can avoid recognizing what I have called 'judgement' as a partner, not only in those abilities we call skills, but in all abilities whatever, and, more particularly, in those abilities which are almost exclusively concerned with mental operations.

The connoisseurship we recognize to belong to the knowledge entailed in riding a horse, for example, or in transmitting or receiving a message in the Morse Code, has its counterpart elsewhere. Indeed, the further we go from manual and sensual skills the larger becomes the place occupied by this component of knowledge. Whatever its place in tea-tasting and in the diagnosis of disease, its place in art and literature, in historical, philosophical or scientific understanding is almost immeasurably greater.

It is represented, for example, in the so-called *divinatio* of the textual critic in which a corrupt reading is detected and an emendation suggested. It is what comes into play where the information to be got from the collation of manuscripts and recension stops. It is all that goes beyond the point where critical rules and methods leave off, and all that is required to drag appropriate precepts from these rules. It is what escapes even the most meticulous list of the qualities required for practising the craft of the textual critic.

A similar ingredient appears in the practical relationships of human beings. The moral and legal rules which set out in propositional form the recognized rights and duties, and the prudential maxims which give some flexibility to those rules, constitute only a small part of the knowledge comprised in the ability to live a civilized life. The precepts themselves require interpretation in respect of persons and circumstances; where there is a conflict between precepts, it cannot be resolved by the application of other rules. 'Casuistry', as it has been said, 'is the grave of moral judgement.'

In short, in every 'ability' there is an ingredient of knowledge which cannot be resolved into information, and in some skills this may be the greater part of the knowledge required for their practice. Moreover, 'abilities' do not exist in the abstract but in individual examples: the norms by which they are recognized are afterthoughts, not categorical imperatives. And each individual example has what may be called a style or idiom of its own which cannot be specified in propositions. Not to detect a man's style is to have missed three-quarters of the meaning of his actions and utterances; and not to have acquired a style is to have shut oneself off from the ability to convey any but the crudest meanings.

What, then, is significant is not the observation that one may know how to speak a language without knowing the rules one is following, but the observation that until one can speak the language in a manner not expressly provided for in the rules, one can maker no significant utterance in it. And, of course, by a 'language' I do not mean merely Latin and Spanish, I mean also the languages of history, philosophy, science and practical life. The rules of art are there, but they do not determine the practice of the art; the rules of understanding are there, but they do not themselves endow us with understanding. They set limits – often telling us only what *not* to do if we wish to speak any of the languages of our civilization; but they provide no prescription for all that must go on in the interval between these limits.

4

The inheritance of human achievements into which the teacher is to initiate his pupil is knowledge; and (on this reading of it) knowledge is to be recognized as manifolds of abilities, in each of which there is a synthesis of 'information' and 'judgement'. What bearing has this view of things upon the activities of learning and teaching – learning which is succeeding to the inheritance, and teaching which is deliberately initiating a pupil into it? I doubt very much whether there are any practical conclusions to be drawn from it for either learners or teachers; but I think it may have some virtue as part of an attempt to understand what is going on in learning and teaching.

It suggests, first, that what I have called the two components of knowledge ('information' and 'judgement') can both be communicated and acquired, but cannot be communicated or acquired separately – at least, not on separate occasions or in separate 'lessons'. This, I think, is certainly true in respect of all the more important abilities and passages in the inheritance, and it is not seriously qualified by the observations that it is possible to communicate and acquire inert information, and that there are some skills in which the component of information is minimal.

But, secondly, it suggests that these two components of knowledge cannot be communicated in the same manner. Indeed, as I understand it, the distinction between 'information' and 'judgement' is a distinction between different manners of communication rather than a dichotomy in what is known; and for me it springs from reflecting upon teaching and learning rather than from reflecting upon the nature of knowledge. Thus teaching may be said to be a twofold activity of communicating 'information' (which I shall call 'instructing') and communicating judgement' (which I shall call 'imparting'); and learning may be said to be a twofold activity of acquiring 'information' and coming to possess judgement'.

The rest of what I have to say concerns this distinction and the understanding it may give of what is going on in learning and teaching.

All teaching has a component of instruction, because all knowledge has a component of information. The teacher as instructor is the deliberate conveyor of information to his pupil.

The facts which compose information are specific, impersonal and mostly to be taken on trust; they are also apt to be hard, isolated, arbitrary and inert. They may be stored in encyclopaedias and dictionaries. Their immediate appeal is not to the pupil's desire to understand, but to his curiosity, his desire not to be ignorant – that is, perhaps, to his vanity. This desire not to be ignorant is, for the most part, satisfied by knowing things in terms of their names and by knowing the signification of words and expressions. From his earliest years the pupil has been used to making such discoveries for himself; he has become accustomed to distinguishing in an elementary way between fact and not-fact – without, of course, knowing the rules he is observing in doing so. For the most part he is used to doing all this as part of the process of coming to be at home in the world he inhabits. Thus, when he falls into the hands of an instructor, he is already familiar with the activity of acquiring information, particularly information for immediate use.

The task of the teacher as instructor is to introduce the pupil to facts which have no immediate practical significance. (If there were no such facts, or if they composed an unimportant part of our inheritance, a teacher would be a luxury rather than a necessity.) And, therefore, his first business is to consider and decide what information to convey to his pupil. This may be decided by circumstances: the Sergeant-Instructor does not have to consider whether

THE VOICE OF LIBERAL LEARNING

or not he shall inform his class about the names and uses of the parts of the bren-gun. But, if it is not decided by such circumstances as these, it is something which falls to the teacher as instructor to consider. What part or parts of our inheritance of information shall be transmitted to his pupil?

His second task is to make the information he has to convey more readily learnable by giving it an organization in which the inertness of its component facts is modified.

The organization provided by an immediate application to the practical life of his pupil is spurious; much of the information he has to convey has no such application and would be corrupted by being turned in this direction. The organization provided by a dictionary or an encyclopaedia is not designed for learning but for the rapid discovery of items of information in response to a recognition of specific ignorance. And the organization of information in terms of the modes of thought, or languages, which are the greatest achievements of civilization, is much too sophisticated for the beginner. In these circumstances, what we have settled for, and what the instructor may be expected to settle for, is the organization of information in terms of the more or less arbitrarily distinguished 'subjects' of a school or university curriculum: geography, Latin, chemistry, arithmetic, 'current affairs' or whatnot. Each of these is an organization of information and not a mode of thought; but each permits facts to begin to reveal their rule-like character (that is, their character as tools to be used in doing, making or understanding) and thus to throw off some of their inertness. Moreover, there is, I think, some positive advantage in devising, for pedagogical purposes, special organizations of information which differ from the significant modes of thought of our civilization. For these modes of thought are not themselves organizations of information; and when one of them appears as a school 'subject' – as, for example, 'philosophy' in the curriculum of a *lycée* – its character is apt to be misrepresented. No great harm may be thought to come from representing 'geography' or even 'Latin' as information to be acquired, but there is something odd about 'philosophy' when it appears as the ability, for example, to remember and rehearse the second proof for the existence of God or what Descartes said about dreams.

There are, I think, two other tasks which obviously fall to the teacher as instructor. First, he has to consider the order in which the information contained in each of these somewhat arbitrary organizations of facts shall be transmitted to his pupil. It is this sort of consideration which goes into devising a syllabus, writing a textbook, or composing the programme of an instructing machine. Second, he has to exercise his pupil in this information so that what has been acquired may be recognized in forms other than those in which it was first acquired, and may be recollected on all the occasions when it is relevant. That is, the instructor has not only to hear his pupils recite the Catechism, the Highway Code, the Capes and Bays, the eight-times multiplication table and the Kings of England, but he has also to see that they can answer questions in which this information is properly used. For the importance of information is the accuracy with which it is learned and the readiness with which it can be recollected and used.

Nevertheless, our inheritance of information is so great that, whatever devices the instructor may use to modify its inertness, much of it must be acquired with only the dimmest notion of how it might be used. No doubt it would be a good thing (as Lichtenberg said) if we could be educated in such a way that everything unclear to us was totally incomprehensible; but this is not possible. Learning begins not in ignorance, but in error. Besides, in acquiring information we may learn something else, other and more valuable than either the information itself or perceiving that it is something to be used. And to understand what this is we must turn from 'information' to 'judgement', from the activity of 'instructing' to the activity of 'imparting'.

Something of what I mean by 'judgement' has begun to appear whenever the pupil perceives that information must be used, and perceives the possibility of irrelevance. Something of this is imparted in the organization of information itself, although these organizations are apt to give a restrictive impression of relevance. It is clear that this is not itself information; it cannot be taught in the way in which information may be conveyed, and it cannot be learned, recollected or forgotten in the way in which information may be learned, recollected and forgotten. But it is clear, also, that this is only an intimation of 'judgement', for there is much more to be noticed which no mere organization of information can impart. To perceive that facts are rules or tools, to perceive that rules are always disjunctive and never categorical, is one thing; to have acquired the ability to use them is another.

'Judgement', then, is that which, when united with information, generates knowledge or 'ability' to do, to make, or to understand and explain. It is being able to think – not to think in no manner in particular, but to think with an appreciation of the considerations which belong to different modes of thought. This, of course, is something which must be *learned*; it does not belong to the pupil by the light of nature, and it is as much a part of our civilized inheritance as the information which is its counterpart. But since learning to think is not acquiring additional information it cannot be pursued in the same way as we add to our stock of information.

Further, 'judgement' may be *taught*; and it belongs to the deliberate enterprise of the teacher to teach it. But, although a pupil cannot be explicitly instructed in how to think (there being, here, no rules), 'judgement' can be taught only in conjunction with the transmission of information. That is to say, it cannot be taught in a separate lesson which is not, for example, a geography, a Latin or an algebra lesson. Thus, from the pupil's point of view, the ability to think is something learned as a by-product of acquiring information; and, from the teacher's point of view, it is something which, if it is taught, must be imparted obliquely in the course of instruction. How this is done is to be understood from considering the character of what has to be imparted.

'Judgement', the ability to think, appears first not in merely being aware that information is to be used, that it is a capital and not a stock, but in the ability to use it – the ability to invest it in answering questions. The rules may have been mastered, the maxims may be familiar, the facts may be available to recollection; but what do they look like in a concrete situation, and how may a concrete situation (an artefact or an understanding) be generated from this information? How does Latin grammar appear in a page from Cicero (whence, indeed, it was abstracted) and how can it be made to generate a page of genuine Latin prose? What do the copybook maxims look like in moral conduct observed, and how can they be made to generate conduct? These are the facts, but what conclusions do they authorize or forbid? This is the literature – the articulate contents, for example, of current knowledge about magnetic effects – but how does a pupil learn to speak the language in which it is written down: the language of science? How does he acquire the connoisseurship which enables him to determine relevance, which allows him to distinguish between different sorts of questions and the different sorts of answers they call for, which emancipates him from crude absolutes and suffers him to give his assent or dissent in graduate terms?

But learning to think is not merely learning how to judge, to interpret and to use information, it is learning to recognize and enjoy the intellectual virtues. How does a pupil learn disinterested curiosity, patience, intellectual honesty, exactness, industry, concentration and doubt? How does he acquire a sensibility to small differences and the ability to recognize intellectual elegance? How does he come to inherit the disposition to submit to refutation? How does he not merely learn the love of truth and justice, but learn it in such a way as to escape the reproach of fanaticism?

And beyond all this there is something more difficult to acquire, but more important than any of it; namely, the ability to detect the individual intelligence which is at work in every utterance, even in those which convey impersonal information. For every significant act or utterance has a style of its own, a personal idiom, an individual manner of thinking of which it is a reflection. This, what I have called style, is the choice made, not according to the rules, but within the area of freedom left by the negative operation of rules. We may listen to what a man has to say, but unless we overhear in it a mind at work and can detect the idiom of thought, we have understood nothing. Art and conduct, science, philosophy and history, these are not modes of thought *defined* by rules; they exist only in personal explorations of territories only the boundaries of which are subject to definition. To have command over the languages of our civilization is, not to know the rules of their grammar, but to have the opportunity of a syntax and a vocabulary, rich in fine distinctions, in which to think for oneself. Learning, then, is acquiring the ability to feel and to think, and the pupil will never acquire these abilities unless he has learned to listen for them and to recognize them in the conduct and utterances of others.

Besides information, then, this is what has to be learned; for this (and not the dead weight of its products) is the real substance of our inheritance – and nothing can be inherited without learning. This is what the teacher has to 'impart' to his pupil, together with whatever information he chooses to convey.

It cannot be *learned* separately; it is never explicitly learned and it is known only in practice; but it may be learned in everything that is learned, in the carpentry shop as well as in the Latin or chemistry lesson. If it is learned, it can never be forgotten, and it does not need to be recollected in order to be enjoyed. It is, indeed, often enough, the residue which remains when all else is forgotten; the shadow of lost knowledge.

It cannot be *taught* separately; it can have no place of its own in a timetable or a curriculum. It cannot be taught overtly, by precept, because it comprises what is required to animate precept; but it may be taught in everything that is taught. It is implanted unobstrusively in the manner in which information is conveyed, in a tone of voice, in the gesture which accompanies instruction, in asides and oblique utterances, and by example. For 'teaching by example', which is sometimes dismissed as an inferior sort of teaching, generating inflexible knowledge because the rules of what is known remain concealed, is emancipating the pupil from the half-utterances of rules by making him aware of a concrete situation. In imitating the example he acquires not merely a model for the particular occasion, but the disposition to recognize everything as an occasion. It is a habit of listening for an individual intelligence at work in every utterance that may be acquired by imitating a teacher who has this habit. And the intellectual virtues may be imparted only by a teacher who really cares about them for their own sake and never stoops to the priggishness of mentioning them. Not the cry, but the rising of the wild duck impels the flock to follow him in flight.

When I consider, as in private duty bound, how I first became dimly aware that there was something else in learning than the acquisition of information, that the way a man thought was more important than what he said, it was, I think, on the occasions when we had before us concrete situations. It was when we had, not an array of historical 'facts', but (for a moment) the facts suspended in an historian's argument. It was on those occasions when we were made to learn by heart, not the declension of *bonus* (which, of course, had to be learned), but a passage of literature, the reflection of a mind at work in a language. It was on those occasions when one was not being talked to but had the opportunity of over-hearing an intelligent conversation.

And if you were to ask me the circumstances in which patience, accuracy, economy, elegance and style first dawned upon me, I would have to say that I did not come to recognize them in literature, in argument or in geometrical proof until I had first recognized them elsewhere; and that I owed this recognition to a Sergeant gymnastics instructor who lived long before the days of 'physical education' and for whom gymnastics was an intellectual art – and I owed it to him, not on account of anything he ever said, but because he was a man of patience, accuracy, economy, elegance and style.

EDUCATION: THE ENGAGEMENT
AND ITS FRUSTRATION

1972

Education in its most general significance may be recognized as a specific transaction which may go on between the generations of human beings in which newcomers to the scene are initiated into the world they are to inhabit. Thus, for example, when in a late-medieval formulation of the duties of human beings there appeared the precept that parents should educate their children, education was being recognized as a moral transaction, something that may (but ought not to) be neglected, and distinguished from the un-avoidable natural processes in which all living things grow up and either accommodate themselves to their circumstances or perish.

Consequently education is recognized as something to be thought about; and in the course of reflection two topics in particu-lar have emerged. The first is concerned to distinguish this transac-tion, to discern what is going on in it, to identify the relationships it involves, in short, to understand it as a specific human engage-ment. The concern here might be said to be with the question 'What is the character of the world which a human newcomer is to inhabit?' The second is the consideration of the procedures, meth-ods and devices believed to be appropriate to the engagement. The second of these topics is clearly subordinate to the first, and all who have thought profoundly about it have recognized this sub-ordination. I shall have little to say about it, except to notice, later on, how in recent times procedures and devices have broken loose from this subordination and have imposed themselves upon our understanding of the transaction itself, with unfortunate consequences. My concern is with the first of these topics. I want to display education as a human engagement of a certain kind and as a transaction upon which a recognizably human life depends for its continuance; and I want, then, to go on to consider some of the obstacles which now hinder and may even frustrate this transaction.

Human beings are what they understand themselves to be; they are composed entirely of beliefs about themselves and about the world they inhabit. They inhabit a world of intelligibles, that is, a world composed, not of physical objects, but of occurrences which have meanings and are recognized in manners to which there are alternatives. Their contingent situations in this world are, therefore, what they understand them to be, and they respond to them by choosing to say or to do *this* rather than *that* in relation to imagined and wished-for outcomes. They are creatures of want. Their wants are not biological impulses or genetic urges; they are imagined satisfactions, which have reasons but not causes, and are eligible to be wished-for, chosen, pursued, procured, approved or disapproved.

A human life is composed of performances, and each performance is a disclosure of a man's beliefs about himself and the world and an exploit in self-enactment. He is what he becomes; he has a history but no 'nature'. This history is not an evolutionary process or a teleological engagement; there is no 'ultimate man' hidden in the womb of time or prefigured in the characters who now walk the world. Human beings pursue satisfactions which they believe to be desirable, but human conduct is not the flowering of a settled potentiality.

The wished-for satisfactions of human beings lie, for the most part, in the responses their utterances and actions receive from others, responses which are themselves utterances and actions related to the wished-for satisfactions of those who make them. Thus, human satisfactions are the outcome of transactions, and to seek them is to enter into a relation with another or with others. These associations are not physical 'interactions' like chemical processes; they are chosen and understood relationships. Human beings do not merely 'communicate' with one another; they speak words which have meanings and are understood (or misunderstood) by those to whom they speak. To hear is to listen, and to listen is to think; and the responses they make to one another are replies or rejoinders governed by the wished-for satisfactions of those who make them. Thus, human conduct subscribes to procedures, but it does not constitute processes. These procedures are not causes which determine what is said or done; they are composed of rules

64

and rule-like considerations to be subscribed to in choosing what to say or to do. They are, moreover, multiple (there is no one comprehensive procedure to correspond to the word 'society' as it is commonly used); and each is an historic achievement which might have been different from what it is and which requires to be understood in order to be used in conduct.

Being human is recognizing oneself to be related to others, not as parts of an organism are related, nor as members of a single, all-inclusive 'society', but in virtue of participation in multiple understood relationships and in the enjoyment of understood, historic languages of feelings, sentiments, imaginings, fancies, desires, recognitions, moral and religious beliefs, intellectual and practical enterprises, customs, conventions, procedures and practices, canons, maxims and principles of conduct, rules which denote obligations and offices which specify duties. These languages are continuously invented by those who share them; using them is adding to their resources. They do not impose demands to think or to 'behave' in a certain manner; they are not sets of ready-made formulae for self-disclosure and self-enactment; they reach those who share them as various invitations to understand, to admire, to approve or to disapprove; and they come only in being learned.

In short, a human being is the inhabitant of a world composed, not of 'things', but of meanings; that is, of occurrences in some manner recognized, identified, understood and responded to in terms of this understanding. It is a world of sentiments and beliefs, and it includes also human artefacts (such as books, pictures, musical compositions, tools and utensils) for these, also, are 'expressions' which have meanings and which require to be understood in order to be used or enjoyed. To be without this understanding is to be, not a human being, but a stranger to a human condition.

Now, I have begun with this characterization of a human life because, if it were not like this, education would be a redundant engagement. If a human life were a process of growth in which a potential became an actual, or if it were a process in which an organism reacted to its circumstances in terms of a genetic equipment, there would be no room for a transaction between the generations designed expressly to initiate a newcomer into what was going on and thus enable him to participate in it. But such is not the case. A human life is composed of performances, choices to do *this* rather than *that* in relation to imagined and wished-for outcomes and governed by beliefs, opinions, understandings, practices, procedures, rules and recognitions of desirabilities and undesirabilities, impossible to engage in merely in virtue of a genetic equipment and without learning to do so. Even the dexterities of human beings have to be learned because they, like everything else in a human life, are governed by desirabilities. For a child to learn to walk is not like a fledgling taking to the air: do I not remember being told to 'walk properly' and not shamble along as if I were an ape? The March Hare's dance and the song of a blackbird may be attributed to genetic urges, but a waltz and *Dove sono* are historic human inventions which have to be learned and understood if they are to be known, enjoyed or responded to. In short, the educational engagement is necessary because nobody is born a human being, and because the quality of being human is not a latency which becomes an actuality in a process of 'growth'. The human newcomer is not an organism in search of an accommodation to circumstances favourable to its continued existence; he is *homo dissens*, a creature capable of learning to think, to understand and to enact himself in a world of human enactments and thus to acquire a human character.

In considering what is going on in this transaction between the generations, then, the first thing to recognize is that it is a transaction between human beings and postulants to a human condition in which newcomers are initiated into an inheritance of human achievements of understanding and belief.

If this inheritance were composed of natural 'things' or artefacts, then its transmission would be hardly more than a mechanical formality, a handing over of physical objects. But it is not. It is composed of human activities, aspirations, sentiments, images, opinions, beliefs, modes of understanding, customs and practices; in short, states of mind which may be entered into only in a procedure of learning.

If this inheritance were merely states of mind, then the initiation might be achieved by hypnosis, by therapy, by means of subcutaneous injections or electric shocks or in so-called 'sleep learning'. But it is not. It is composed of states of mind which, because they constitute understandings, can be enjoyed only by virtue of their being themselves understood. To be human is to engage in activities knowing what you are doing, and consequently initiation into this condition can be only in an engagement in which the newcomer learns to understand.

What is going on in this transaction, then, is not the transfer of the products of earlier generations to a newcomer, nor is it a newcomer acquiring an aptitude for imitating current adult human performances; it is learning to perform humanly. Education is not acquiring a stock of ready-made ideas, images, sentiments, beliefs and so forth; it is learning to look, to listen, to think, to feel, to imagine, to believe, to understand, to choose and to wish. It is a postulant to a human condition learning to recognize himself as a human being in the only way in which this is possible: namely, by seeing himself in the mirror of an inheritance of human understandings and activities and thus himself acquiring (in the words of Leibniz) the character of *un miroir vivant, doué d'action interne*, acquiring the ability to throw back upon the world his own version of a human being in conduct which is both a self-disclosure and a self-enactment.

This transaction between the generations will, however, be inhibited unless there is a contingent belief in the worth of what is to be mediated to the newcomer, and unless this conviction is somehow also transmitted. Everything human exists in terms of the recognition of its desirability, and this civilized inheritance, this world of meanings and understandings, will be transmitted only where it inspires the gratitude, the pride and even the veneration of those who already enjoy it, where it endows them with an identity they esteem, and where it is understood as a repeated summons rather than a possession, an engagement rather than an heirloom.

I am not concerned with that mysterious accommodation to the world which constitutes the early history of a human being; activity emerging imperceptibly and intermittently from passivity; movements becoming actions; urges giving place to wants and wants to choices; presentations becoming representations, remembered, recollected, recognized and gradually identified; occurrences coming to be recognized as events; 'things' emerging from characteristics; 'objects' perceived as signs and signs revealing alternative significances; sounds coming to be recognized as words with meanings determined by contexts; human procedures distinguished from natural processes – all the fluctuations which go on in the morning twilight of childhood, where there is nothing that, at a given moment, a clever child may be said exactly to know or not to know.

At home in the nursery or in the kindergarten, in the early years of childhood, attention and activity, when they begin to be self-moved, are, for the most part, ruled by inclination; the self is inclination. Things and occurrences (even when they have been expressly designed or arranged by adults) are gifts of fortune known only in terms of what can be made of them. Everything is an opportunity, recognized and explored for the immediate satisfaction it may be made to yield. Learning, here, is a by-product of play; what is learned is what may happen to be learned.

But education, properly speaking, begins when, upon these casual encounters provoked by the contingencies of moods, upon these fleeting wants and sudden enthusiasms tied to circumstances, there supervenes the deliberate initiation of a newcomer into a human inheritance of sentiments, beliefs, imaginings, understandings and activities. It begins when the transaction becomes 'schooling' and when learning becomes learning by study, and not by chance, in conditions of direction and restraint. It begins with the appearance of a teacher with something to impart which is *not* immediately connected with the current wants or 'interests' of the learner.

The idea 'School' is, in the first place, that of a serious and orderly initiation into an intellectual, imaginative, moral and emotional inheritance; an initiation designed for children who are ready to embark upon it. Superimposed upon these chance encounters with fragments of understanding, these moments of unlooked-for enlightenment and those answers imperfectly understood because they are answers to unasked questions, there is a considered curriculum of learning to direct and contain the thoughts of the learner, to focus his attention and to provoke him to distinguish and to discriminate. 'School' is the recognition that the first and most important step in education is to become aware that 'learning' is not a 'seamless robe', that possibilities are not limitless.

Secondly, it is an engagement to learn by study. This is a difficult undertaking; it calls for effort. Whereas playful occupations are broken off whenever they cease to provide immediate satisfactions, learning, here, is a task to be persevered with and what is learned has to be both understood and remembered. It is in this perseverance, this discipline of inclination, that the indispensable habits of attention, concentration, patience, exactness, courage and intellectual honesty are acquired, and the learner comes to recognize that difficulties are to be surmounted, not evaded. For example, in a profuse and complicated civilization such as our own, the inheritance of human understandings, modes of thinking, feeling and imagination is to be encountered, for the most part, in books or in human utterances. But learning to read or to listen is a slow and exacting engagement, having little or nothing to do with acquiring information. It is learning to follow, to understand and to rethink deliberate expressions of rational consciousness; it is learning to recognize fine shades of meaning without overbalancing into the lunacy of 'decoding'; it is allowing another's thoughts to re-enact themselves in one's own mind; it is learning in acts of constantly surprised attention to submit to, to understand and to respond to what (in this response) becomes a part of our understanding of ourselves; and one may learn to read only by reading with care, and only from writings which stand well off from our immediate concerns: it is almost impossible to *learn* to read from contemporary writing.

The third component of the idea 'School' is that of detachment from the immediate, local world of the learner, its current concerns and the directions it gives to his attention, for this (and not 'leisure' or 'play') is the proper meaning of the word *schole*. 'School' is a place apart in which the heir may encounter his moral and intellectual inheritance, not in the terms in which it is being used in the current engagements and occupations of the world outside (where much of it is forgotten, neglected, obscured, vulgarized or abridged, and where it appears only in scraps and as investments in immediate enterprises) but as an estate, entire, unqualified and unencumbered. 'School' is an emancipation achieved in a continuous redirection of attention. Here, the learner is animated, not by the inclinations he brings with him, but by intimations of excellence and aspirations he has never yet dreamed of; here he may encounter, not answers to the 'loaded' questions of 'life', but questions which have never before occurred to him; here he may acquire new 'interests' and pursue them uncorrupted by the need for immediate results; here he may learn to seek satisfactions he had never yet imagined or wished for.

For example, an important part of this inheritance is composed of languages, and in particular of what is to be the native language of the newcomer. This he has already learned to speak in its contemporary idioms and as a means of communicating with others of his kind. But at 'School' he learns something more which is also something different. There, studying a language is recognizing words as investments in thought and is learning to think more exactly; it is exploring its resources as themselves articulations of understandings. For to know a language merely as a means of contemporary communication is to be like a man who has inherited a palace overflowing with expressions, intimations and echoes of human emotions, perceptions, aspirations and understandings, and furnished with images and emanations of human reflection, but in whose barbaric recognition his inheritance is merely that of 'a roof over his head'. In short, 'School' is 'monastic' in respect of being a place apart where excellences may be heard because the din of worldly laxities and partialities is silenced or abated.

Further, the idea 'School' is that of a personal transaction between a 'teacher' and a 'learner'. The only indispensable equipment of 'School' is teachers: the current emphasis on apparatus of all sorts (not merely 'teaching' apparatus) is almost wholly destructive of 'School'. A teacher is one in whom some part or aspect or passage of this inheritance is alive. He has something of which he is a master to impart (an ignorant teacher is a contradiction) and he has deliberated its worth and the manner in which he is to impart it to a learner whom he knows. He is himself the custodian of that 'practice' in which an inheritance of human understanding survives and is perpetually renewed in being imparted to newcomers. To teach is to bring it about that, somehow, something of worth intended by a teacher is learned, understood and remembered by a learner. Thus, teaching is a variegated activity which may include hinting, suggesting, urging, coaxing, encouraging, guiding, pointing out, conversing, instructing, informing, narrating, lecturing, demonstrating, exercising, testing, examining, criticizing, correcting, tutoring, drilling and so on – everything, indeed, which does not belie the engagement to impart an understanding. And learning may be looking, listening, overhearing, reading, receiving suggestions, submitting to guidance, committing to memory, asking questions, discussing, experimenting, practising, taking notes, recording, re-expressing and so on – anything which does not belie the engagement to think and to understand.

Finally, the idea 'School' is that of an historic community of teachers and learners, neither large nor small, with traditions of its own, evoking loyalties, pieties and affections; devoted to initiating successive generations of newcomers to the human scene into the grandeurs and servitudes of being human; an Alma Mater who remembers with pride or indulgence and is remembered with gratitude. The marks of a good school are that in it learning may be recognized as, itself, a golden satisfaction with needs no adventitious gilding to recommend it; and that it bestows upon its alumni the gift of a childhood recollected, not as a passage of time hurried through on the way to more profitable engagements, but, with gratitude, as an enjoyed initiation into the mysteries of a human condition: the gift of self-knowledge and of a satisfying intellectual and moral identity.

Thus, this transaction between the generations cannot be said to have any extrinsic 'end' or 'purpose': for the teacher it is part of his engagement of being human; for the learner it is the engagement of becoming human. It does not equip the newcomer to do anything specific; it gives him no particular skill, it promises no material advantage over other men, and it points to no finally perfect human character. Each, in participating in this transaction, takes in keeping some small or large part of an inheritance of human understandings. This is the mirror before which he enacts his own version of a human life, emancipated from the modishness of merely current opinions and released from having to seek an exiguous identity in a fugitive fancy, a duffle-coat, a CND badge or an 'ideology'. Education is not learning to do *this* or *that* more proficiently; it is acquiring in some measure an understanding of a human condition in which the 'fact of life' is continuously illuminated by a 'quality of life'. It is learning how to be at once an autonomous and a civilized subscriber to a human life.

Now, this is not a merely fanciful or visionary characterization of education. Of course, in the long history of the apprenticeship of newcomers to an adult human life other ideas than this of education have often intruded. Peoples with less complex inheritances of beliefs and understandings have had appropriately simpler notions of this transaction between the generations, and, of course, there are and have been better and worse schools, and better and worse periods in the history of any school. But what I have been describing is what the ancient Athenians understood as *paideia*; and, sometimes more narrowly and sometimes more generously, it was what was passed on (with appropriate changes) from the schools of the Roman Empire to the cathedral, the collegiate, guild and grammar schools of medieval Christendom. Moved by a vivid consciousness of an intellectual and moral inheritance of great splendour and worth, this was the notion of education which informed the schools of renaissance Europe and which survived in our own grammar and public schools and their equivalents in continental Europe.

In later times, however, this understanding and practice of education has been invaded from two somewhat different directions. In both cases the forces of invasion have been gathering themselves over a period of some centuries, and both have been rewarded with considerable temporary success. Their common enterprise is to substitute for education some other and almost totally different idea of apprenticeship to adult life, and for 'School' some other and almost totally different practice of initiation.

The first of these invasions is to be recognized as an assault upon education directed against the idea 'School'. It is designed to abolish 'School', first by corrupting it and then by suppressing it.

The engagement to educate is a transaction between the generations in which newcomers may enjoy what they can acquire only in a procedure of learning; namely, an historic inheritance of human understandings and imaginings. The idea 'School' is that of a place apart where a prepared newcomer may encounter this inheritance unqualified by the partialities, the neglects, the abridgements and the corruptions it suffers in current use; of an engagement to learn, not by chance, but by study in conditions of direction and restraint designed to provoke habits of attention, concentration, exactness, courage, patience, discrimination and the recognition of excellence in thought and conduct; and of an apprenticeship to adult life in which he may learn to recognize and identify himself in terms other than those of his immediate circumstances.

The doctrine we are now to consider is that for all this there should be substituted an arena of childish self-indulgence from which all that might contain impulse and inclination and turn them into deliberate and knowledgeable choice has been purposely removed: a place where a child may be as rude as his impulses prompt and as busy or as idle as his inclinations suggest. There is to be no curriculum of study, no orderly progression in learning. Impulse is to be let loose upon an undifferentiated confusion called, alternatively, 'the seamless robe of learning' or 'life in all its manifestations'. What may be learned is totally unforeseen and a matter of complete indifference.

Each child is expected to engage in such individual projects of so-called 'experimental' activity as he feels inclined, to pursue them in his own way and for so long as his inclination to do so lasts. Learning is to be a personal 'finding out' and consequently it becomes the incidental, exiguous and imperfectly understood by-product of 'discovery'. To 'discover' nothing is to be preferred to being told anything. The child is to be shielded from the humiliation (as it is thought) of his own ignorance and of intellectual surprise, and sheltered in the unfrustrating womb of his own inclinations. Teaching is to be confined to hesitant (preferably wordless) suggestion; mechanical devices are to be preferred to teachers, who are recognized not as custodians of a deliberate procedure of initiation but as mute presences, as interior decorators who arrange the furnishings of an environment and as mechanics to attend to the audio-visual apparatus.

'Discoveries' may become the subjects of 'free' group discussions; or they may be written about in compositions to be esteemed, not on account of their intelligibility, but for their 'freedom' of expression. It does not matter how they are written so long as they are 'creative': to stutter independently is a superior accomplishment to that of acquiring the self-discipline of a mother tongue. Fancy will have no encouragement to flower into imagination, or impulsive expression to acquire the intellectual virtue of grace, let alone exactness. Seeing and doing are preferred to thinking and understanding; pictorial representation is preferred to speech or writing. Remembering, the nursing mother of learning, is despised as a relic of servility. Standards of understanding and conduct are not merely ignored; they are taboo. The so-called 'inner discipline' of impulse, coupled with persuasion and physical intervention, takes the place of rules of conduct. In short, 'School' is to be corrupted by having imposed upon it the characteristics of a very indifferent kindergarten: 'Secondary schools', it is announced, 'will follow the lead already taken by primary schools'.

Now, it may be doubted whether anything exactly like this exists. What we have to consider is not a current practice, but a doctrine now loudly preached by persons in positions of authority.

Many of the writers who believe this condition of things to be both desirable and unavoidable are of no account. They affect to believe that 'School' as a deliberate initiation of a learner into an inheritance of human understandings and proprieties of conduct is, and must be, children condemned to a prison-like existence in cell-like classrooms, compelled by threats to follow a sordid, senseless and rigid routine which destroys all individuality, dragooned into learning what they do not and cannot understand because it is remote from their 'interests' and from what they have hitherto encountered, the victims of a conspiracy against 'life' who acquiesce in their degraded condition only because to revolt would be to forfeit the subsequent opportunity of profitable employment. A voluble revulsion from this delusion, eked out by rubbish about the 'pursuit of truth' and what purports to be a superior understanding of the current generation of children, is all that these writers have to sustain their pretence of having thought about education.

There are, however, others who have (or who are reputed to have) more substantial reasons for promoting this abolition of 'School'. There are, for example, those for whom *any* inheritance of human understandings, so far from being something to be esteemed and which should evoke gratitude and make a child glad to be alive and eager to become human, is an insufferable burden. 'I say to myself,' writes one such would-be exile from the human condition, 'What happiness it would be to throw myself into the river Lethe, to erase completely from my soul the memory of all knowledge, all art, all poetry; what happiness it would be to reach the opposite shore, naked, like the first man.'

It seems appropriate that such a person should see in education and in 'School' (however well managed) nothing but a frustrating intrusion upon blessed innocence, proper only to be abolished and replaced by the 'experimental' activity of unguided explorers with virgin intelligences. But this is an illusion. This aspiration, so elaborately expressed in terms of a recollected human mythology, is itself an historic human sentiment. What is being celebrated here is not a wish to be released from an inheritance of human under standings, but a sentiment which is one of the most moving and most delicate components of our inheritance of human understand ings: that tender nostalgia at the heart of all European poetry, that image of impossible release, which we encounter only in being educated. What is being expressed is an understanding of the hu man condition which could never itself be a reason for abolishing education.

A more modish defence of this enterprise to abolish 'School' springs, not from the belief that *any* inheritance of human under standing must be frustrating, but from the persuasion that what is alleged to be the only significant inheritance we have (namely, that which is called 'scientific knowledge') is both so recent and in process of such rapid transformation that 'to cram children with this formal body of knowledge which will quickly become antique' is clearly a lost endeavour. Where there is no 'relevant' inheritance of human understandings, where yesterday's frontier of knowledge is tomorrow's rubbish-dump of ideas, when we are in the middle of a technological revolution where skills and standards of conduct are evanescent, there is no room for learning which is not 'creative enquiry' or for 'education' which is not an engagement to solve a technological problem. 'School', no doubt, was appropriate enough for those obliged to seek understanding from their an cestors, but now both education and 'School' are anachronisms: there is nothing to learn.

But this enterprise of abolishing 'School' is not a new adventure, and these aspirations and announcements do less than justice to its antiquity and to the beliefs in terms of which it is defended. The current notion that 'School' and education should be replaced by an apprenticeship to adult life in which the newcomer is engaged in an activity of 'discovery' and 'finding out' for himself is the some what tattered relic of the error that the only inheritance which one generation has to transmit to the next is an inheritance of inform ation about 'things' conveyed in words, and that it is, on this ac count, to be mistrusted.

Knowledge, so the doctrine ran, derives solely from the exper ience and observation of 'things'; and it represents 'the empire of man over things'. And where it is knowledge about ourselves, it is not a moral understanding of the 'dignity' of man, but knowledge of psychophysical processes. This knowledge is recorded in words, and in words it is passed on. No great damage would be done if these words were always accurate reports about 'things', but for the most part this is not the case; words are distorting images of 'things' and they corrupt the information they purport to convey. 'Words obstruct understanding.' If, then, we are in earnest about knowledge, it is 'solid things', and not words, which should be 'the objects of our attention'. 'The first distemper of learning is when men study words and not things.' If we are concerned to educate, we must not try to convey our observations to others in words, for 'knowledge ought to be delivered and insinuated by the same method whereby it was achieved', namely, by an enquirer engaging for himself in the observation of 'things' and making his own discoveries. Morever, this is not only the proper way of learning, it also holds out the promise of genuine discovery; for important 'discoveries' are often made accidentally by people of no great intelligence: they may come to a child following an impulse to 'find out'.[1]

I have been quoting from the writings of Francis Bacon, who may be recognized as the father of this project to abolish 'School'. Indeed, it is not without interest that he did his best to prevent the foundation of what became a famous school, The Charterhouse, on the ground that it would concern itself, like other grammar schools, with the misconceived engagement of initiating new generations of boys into an inheritance of human understandings. There is, of course, much in Bacon's writings besides this doctrine, and something to modify it; but at that now distant date there was set on foot, not merely a suggestion which might be recognized as a valuable addition to our methods of educating the very young (for example, 'encourage children to look and to touch'), but this misunderstanding of the educational engagement itself, with its often quoted slogan 'Things, not words',[2] with its taciturn teacher, its erroneous belief that 'language is but the instrument conveying to us things useful to be known', its total neglect of literature, its absence of curriculum, its accent on crude information, its elevation of inclination, its pragmatic aspirations and with its conviction that a man's identity is to be found, not in his relation to an inheritance of

---

[1] 'The student with an external vocational referent for his studies always has the possible justification for his most outrageous ideas – that they work.' E. E. Robinson, *The New Polytechnics* (London: Cornmarket, 1968).

[2] This nearly meaningless expression, which runs through the history of modern so-called educational theory, has done more than anything else to corrupt our understanding of the educational engagement.

human understandings, sentiments and beliefs, but in relation to a world of 'solid things' – all of which I have identified as the first of the current projects for the abolition of 'School' and the destruction of education.

In the doctrine of Bacon and his near contemporaries, Comenius, Hartlib, Milton *et al.*, 'education' stood, not for a transaction between the generations of human beings in which the newcomer was initiated into an inheritance of human understandings, sentiments, imaginings, and so forth, but for a release from all this in which he acquired 'objective' knowledge of the workings of a 'natural' world of uncontaminated 'things' and 'laws' and of himself as a feature of this world. This doctrine was early embalmed in a set of clichés, the repetition of which over the succeeding centuries constituted one of the 'progressive' strains in modern educational theory. It made no immediate impact upon the educational engagement of European peoples, but it emerged later as the rationale of a design to abolish education.

But the current invaders of the educational engagement do not stop at this project to corrupt schools by depriving them of their character as 'School'; they design and foresee their suppression.

The more hesitant of these reformers imagine the dissolution of schools in terms of a dissolution of the distinction between 'School' and the world outside. Their moderate vision embraces merely the abolition of the child and of 'School' as a place apart. What is to take its place is a 'community centre', a combination of a local parliament, a people's court, a village hall, an information centre, a clinic, a social guidance organization, a sports club, an amusement park, a polytechnic and a 'cultural centre'. Hither, children and adults will repair when they feel inclined to do so. There they may together exercise their inclinations and their impulsive energies which, in the case of children, will have 'burst out of the classroom box'. There, at the age of twelve or thereabouts, and emancipated from the alleged superstition that knowledge is diverse, they will become equal participants in the local world of adult activities and win their 'education' from the open book of life. In this community centre the child-adult will find, not teachers, but 'trained social workers'; he will find a 'structured environment' which will provide endless opportunity for 'self-expression' and for making unforeseen 'discoveries'; and rooms equipped with 'technological devices', programmed teaching machines and apparatus to relay pictures and talks, broadcast from a central School of the Air. There, a stranger to duties, relieved from frustration, allegedly emancipated from the 'intrusion of adult interference', he will enjoy a self-determined 'education', limited only by the decreed exclusion of any alternative. For, of course, this suppression of 'School' will come about only in a dissolution of schools comparable to the dissolution of monasteries in sixteenth-century Europe; it will be the work of 'enlightened' governments.

Others have seen beyond this still homely vision of an amusement arcade and playground for all ages. Inspired by the promise held out by recent mechanical invention, they foresee a future in which each home will become 'the basic learning unit'. It will contain 'an electronic console connected with a central computer system, a videotape and a microfilm library regulated by a computer, and with a national television network'. All 'education' will be dispensed from a 'central educational hub'. No longer will children have to 'go to school', or have 'to jostle their way into class'. Each child, at the touch of a button, will have access to a 'learning package' programmed for individual use. He will 'type on a surface resembling a television screen in response to recorded instructions regulated by a computer'; and, 'at the touch of a button, "teachers" may call up profiles of his progress and advise accordingly'. He will be able 'to choose his own educational goals' and pursue them at his own pace.

But the residual recognition of education which survives in these proposals or forecasts is absent from the plans of the most intrepid of our 'educational' projectors, who look forward to a final dissolution of both 'School' and schools. They design not merely the abolition of the child but the abolition of man. The child who asks himself 'What shall I learn and where is the machine to teach me'? is to be replaced by the social engineer concerned with the question 'What sort of a "human being" do we want and how may he be most easily manufactured'? 'The possibilities', writes one of these visionaries, 'virtually defy our imagination'. Here, in spite of the claim to be concerned with education, any pretence of teaching, learning or understanding has been abandoned. Desirable children will be the outcome of controlled genetic selection, and their 'behaviour' will be determined by brains stimulated by electrical currents and by the injection of extracts from other more distinguished brains, by inoculation with chemicals and by other irresistible processes of conditioning. With the emergence of this race of zombies, who behave impeccably, who are strangers to neuroses, plagued by no frustrations, unworried about their own identities (because they need none), but who can neither understand nor act, 'Man's best dreams', says this same professor of education, 'seem almost within our grasp'.

To corrupt 'School' by depriving it of its character as a serious engagement to learn by study, and to abolish it either by assimilating it to the activities, 'interests', partialities and abridgments of a local world, or by substituting in its place a factory for turning out zombies, are, then, two sides of the current project to destroy education. It is an enterprise for abolishing man, first by disinheriting him, and secondly by annihilating him. That some of the persons engaged in this enterprise should represent their doctrine as an improved understanding of the educational engagement, and that they should claim to be the friends and emancipators of children, is not unexpected; but the representation is false and the claim fraudulent.

But, although this enterprise and the doctrines which support it are the most carefully contrived of the current projects to abolish the educational engagement, they do not exhaust the current threat to education. I will conclude with a brief consideration of another enterprise which has increasingly hindered this engagement and now threatens to obliterate it.

The engagement to educate may be frustrated by the conviction that there is no inheritance of human understandings and beliefs into which to initiate a newcomer; or by the belief that there is such an inheritance, but that, since it is necessarily worthless, the apprenticeship of each new generation to adult life should be a ceremonial rejection of what it would be corrupting even to inspect, followed by 'a disturbed and disturbing argument of a creative kind' in which each generation originates its own understandings, governed (one must suppose) by a self-denying ordinance not to inhibit 'progress' by divulging it to the next.

It may, however, also be hindered (and indeed, in an important respect, utterly frustrated) by the belief that, although there may be a considerable inheritance of human understandings, sentiments, beliefs, etc., in terms of which a newcomer might be released from the grip of his immediate world and come to understand and identify himself as a civilized human being aware of standards of excellence in thought and conduct little or not at all reflected in the current enterprises and activities of that world, this identity is both distracting and 'socially dangerous'. It distracts from the ordinary business of life and, since it is an identity not equally attainable by all, it is more apt to be socially 'divisive' than integrative. Hence, the apprenticeship of the newcomer to adult life should be an initiation, not into the *grandeurs* of human understanding, but into the skills, activities and enterprises which constitute the local world into which he is presently and actually born. The postulant to adult life is bidden to seek himself and to learn to enact himself in terms of an assigned or a self-chosen role in an association of *fonctionnaires*.

This I will call the substitution of 'socialization' for education. It is to be a recognized as a frustration of the educational engagement and a destruction of 'School' because it attributes to the teaching and learning which compose this apprenticeship an extrinsic 'end' or 'purpose'; namely, the integration of the newcomer into a current 'society' recognized as the manifold of skills, activities, enterprises, understandings, sentiments and beliefs required to keep it going; in short, 'to rear the most "current" men possible, "current" in the sense in which the word is used of coins of the realm'.[3] It may be recognized as a different frustration of the educational engagement from those which I have already noticed; although, of course, there may be contingent connections between them.

The belief that what I have called 'socialization' should be substituted for education is to be distinguished, first, from the belief that we live in societies which, because they are associations of human beings, depend upon their members being human, that is, being in some degree educated persons. For, to believe this is not to attribute an extrinsic 'purpose' to the engagement in which these persons acquire a human character; 'being human', here, is recognized, not as a means to an end (i.e. living with other human beings), but as a condition for which it is meaningless to ask for a justification in respect of human beings. What else should they be? Second, it must be distinguished from the recognition that the qualities of educated persons may often be valuable in the performance of 'social' functions. For, while an educational engagement is not designed to *produce* performers of 'social' functions (this is what is meant by saying it has no extrinsic 'purpose'), neither is it designed to *produce* 'socially' valueless persons.

The enterprise we are concerned with now may be most accurately described as that of substituting 'social' for educational consideration in the apprenticeship of newcomers to adult life. Of course, this substitution of one set of considerations for another is hostile to the educational engagement and to the idea 'School', not because it necessarily excludes everything which might have an educational value, but because whatever is allowed properly to belong to this apprenticeship is admitted solely in respect of its alleged 'social' value and is recognized solely in relation to an alleged 'social' purpose. 'Service to the community' is an expression susceptible of a variety of interpretations in relation to 'education' – it

---

[3] Nietzsche, *Über die Zukunft unserer Bildungsanstalten*, I.

may favour rare ability or commonplace equality – but wherever preparation for it is substituted for education 'socialization' has taken the place of the educational engagement.

The current project of substituting 'socialization' for education and instruments of 'socialization' for schools emerged, so far as Europe is concerned, from a somewhat different enterprise, promoted or undertaken, for the most part, by the rulers of modern European states beginning in the late seventeenth century. What I refer to here is not the activities of these rulers (both Catholic and Protestant) in respect of the educational engagement itself when, beginning in the sixteenth century, they gradually usurped the *auctoritas docendi* of the medieval church. These activities were often extensive and were, of course, designed to promote the integration of those over whom they ruled. They included the imposition of confessional qualifications upon both teachers and learners in schools and universities, but they did not otherwise seriously modify the educational engagement. They were, for the most part, the exercise of the ecclesiastical authority which had fallen to civil sovereign, and the many schools and universities founded at this time under royal or ducal charters or by private benefactors were institutions similar to those which already existed. They were novel only in reflecting the changes in the educational engagement which sprang from the 'new learning', changes concerned with the new appreciation (afoot since the fifteenth century) of the significant inheritance of human understandings to be passed on. Furthermore, in later times governments have acquired extensive control over the education of their subjects, over the curriculum of schools and the appointment of teachers, but without imposing considerations hostile to the educational engagement and to the idea 'School'. What I am concerned with now is not any of this, but a project which lies to one side of it; namely, the provision of an *alternative* to education.

In many of the States of Germany (notably Prussia), in France, in the British Empire and elsewhere, what was set on foot in the early eighteenth century was not any attempt to change the character of existing schools and universities, nor to modify the educational engagement; it was the project of providing some alternative apprenticeship to adult life for those who, mainly by reason of their poverty, enjoyed little or nothing of the kind. These, the *canaille*, as the 'enlightened' rulers of continental Europe so gracefully called them, were coming to be regarded as a liability. Stuck fast in traditional ways, outflanked by economic and technological change, unable to provide successfully for themselves, they were convicted of making an inadequate contribution to the productive enterprise of the societies into which they were born. The project was to equip their children with some humble but more modern skills by virtue of which they might become an asset rather than a liability to 'the nation'. They were to be taught to read, to write, to figure, to measure, to 'take directions', to read and to draw diagrams, to understand transactions in money, and religious instruction was usually added to this curriculum. Thus furnished, it was thought that they would be able to make a larger contribution to the well-being of 'the nation' and begin to recognize themselves more clearly as intelligent components of its natural resources, its 'human capital'. It was even recognized that a totally ignorant soldier was something of a liability, and the standing armies of the Continent at that time were large. Moreover, this undertaking to 'integrate' the poor into 'the community' by equipping them to be more useful members of it was seen to promise a national system of so-called 'education', an *education publique* or an *education nationale*, itself the emblem of the emergent doctrine that rulers have a right to instruct their subjects and that subjects (particularly the poor) have a duty to contribute to the well-being of 'the nation'.[4] In England there was a similar recognition of the waste of resources entailed in the ignorance of the poor, but this sort of instruction had been unevenly provided since the late seventeenth century in parish and charity schools and in schools set up or taken over by such organizations as the Society for Promoting Christian Knowledge and later the National Society. It was not until later that the Government began to play some part in it, and even then the continental doctrine that children (especially poor children) belong to 'the State' was slow to take root.

Thus, parallel to the collegiate and grammar schools of England and to their equivalents on the Continent, there emerged an apprenticeship to adult life distinguished both by its brevity and because it was governed by 'social', not educational, considerations. It was geared to satisfying what were already thought of as 'the needs of the nation', and the well-being of 'the nation' was recognized to require that this instruction of the children of the poor should be appropriate to their future occupations. The institutions in which this instruction was dispensed were, everywhere, a mixture of new and old and reflected local inheritances. This alternative to education emerged from the surviving village schools of

---

[4] Hobbes had earlier suggested that this alternative for education should be devoted merely to teaching the duty of 'obedience' to the civil sovereign.

medieval Christendom which had depended upon the uncertainties of local charity and the energy of the parish priest, and, no doubt, it long remained subject to these hazards. But it emerged clearly when, usually under the direction of a ruler, these were diminished, when attendance was made compulsory and when its extrinsic purpose was more exactly understood and formulated.

This alternative to education, designed originally for the poor and as an undertaking of 'socialization', was, of course, sensitive to 'social' changes, and with the emergence of industrial occupations it was considerably extended. In England, for example, in the early nineteenth century, besides the parish and charity schools, there appeared private schools and 'academies' established to provide, not for the poor, but for the numerous postulants for the clerkly and other occupations of an industrial and commercial society; and since that time there has gradually emerged, in every European country, as an alternative to education, a systematic apprenticeship to domestic, industrial and commercial life in a 'modern' State.

It has been continuously thought about, rearranged, redesigned and improved. It has been enlarged in response to new 'needs'; the period of time it covers has been extended and the qualifications it confers have become more precise and require to be earned in more exacting achievements. But its general character has remained unchanged. There is now, in most European countries, a primary stage in which literacy and numeracy are learned and practised; a second stage in which these accomplishments are extended and some general knowledge (particularly what is called 'scientific' knowledge) is acquired; and a third stage in which some specialized skill or technique is learned in an apprenticeship, a Trade School, a Technical College, a Polytechnic or a private establishment where attendance may be full-time or in the intervals of employment. It has come now to embrace nearly all the skills, techniques, crafts, trades and occupations in which the 'needs of the nation' are satisfied. During the last fifty years or so the whole of it (and not merely the earlier stages) has fallen more and more under the direction and control of governments; and in so far as this has been the case it has become susceptible to the sort of calculation entailed in a 'manpower budget' where 'the nation' is understood as a collection of interlocking skills and occupations each with its optimum establishment. Since it has long ago ceased to be merely the equipment of the neglected poor to make a greater and more various contribution to the well-being of 'the nation', other reasons have had to be found in terms of which to defend and to make intelligible this alternative to education, especially its second stage.

For the most part these have drawn upon the beliefs that the 'needs of the nation' can be satisfied in no other way and that there are children for whom the ardours of education would be an unprofitable engagement; but in some quarters these have been supplemented by the assertion that this is itself education and not an alternative to it.

This apprenticeship to domestic, industrial and commercial life was, in its beginning, independent of the educational engagement being pursued in schools and universities. There were, of course, connections between them. Many of the entrants to grammar schools (and, before the invention of 'preparatory' schools, to collegiate schools) came from 'petty' and parish schools, and both in Germany and in France the *Gymnasia* and the *lycées* drew their pupils from the *Gemeinder* and the *communaux* schools. Those who supplied what were distinguished as the 'professional' needs of 'the nation' (lawyers, doctors and so forth), as well as many who engaged in industry or commerce, were persons who qualified for their profession or who learned their trade after having been to school and perhaps university. But little of this was reflected in the educational engagement itself: the appearance of an 'Army class' or a 'mathematical side' was an insignificant modification.

Moreover, in spite of its 'social' design, the alternative to education was never totally devoid of educational features. In its beginning, when it was concerned with children up to the age of about eleven, perhaps the only significant element of culture it contained, the only suggestion it made to those who enjoyed it that they might recognize themselves as something more and other than potential units in what was coming to be thought of as a 'productive system', was the religious instruction, frowned upon in France, but elsewhere part of the curriculum. This catechetical teaching cannot have been very inspiring, but it at least intimated an identity and a 'quality of life' beyond the 'fact of life'; in biblical stories something like an inheritance of human understandings was at least dimly to be discerned; and for many the Bible was the only 'literature' they were acquainted with. Long ago this 'primary' stage became the main field of educational experiment which has had the ambiguous outcome of making it, in most European countries, both more and less appropriate as a preparation for 'School'. Similarly, when the period of time covered by the second stage of this apprenticeship to adult life was somewhat extended,[5] its 'socially' designed curri-

---

[5] In England, even in the early nineteenth century, some of the schools of the National Society and other educational organizations provided for children up to the age of fourteen; and where this was so, foreign languages and even some Latin were sometimes taught.

culum acquired some features which, although they might be there for 'social' reasons, held some promise of being educational; for example, a glimpse of the current myth of the history of the nation.

Our concern, however, is not with whatever tenuous educational features there may have been in this historic alternative to education (the second stage of which, so far as England is concerned, was re-examined by the Hadow Committee in 1926)[6] but with the invasion which the educational engagement as it has existed in the schools and universities of Europe has suffered from this alternative. For, after a brief but not wholly ineffective attempt to extend the opportunity of education to more of those who had not hitherto enjoyed it, this has become the most notable feature of the recent history of European 'education': the enterprise of *substituting* 'socialization' for education.[7]

By 'socialization' (let me repeat) I mean here an apprenticeship to adult life – teaching, training, instructing, imparting knowledge, learning, etc. – governed by an extrinsic purpose. The most common version of this alternative to education has been that which emerged from the efforts of rulers and others to equip the poor to make a more effective contribution to the well-being of 'the nation', and which has since been elaborated into more or less systematic arrangements for imparting to successive generations the knowledge and the skills required to sustain the enterprises and provide the satisfactions characteristic of a modern industrial and commercial society. Here the project of substituting 'socialization' for education is that of imposing upon the educational engagement the considerations which comprise this extrinsic purpose. The other notable version of a 'social' alternative to education is a more recent appearance and pulls in a different direction, namely, that of an apprenticeship to adult life governed by the 'social' consideration that it shall be the same for all children. The design here is

---

[6] It will be remembered that the terms of reference of the Hadow Committee required it to consider what had come to be called 'secondary education', that is, a 'post-primary' alternative to education up to the age of fifteen. Every page of the Report (and not least its historical review) shows its concern with an apprenticeship to adult life which should be agreeable to those who were to enjoy it in reflecting the 'interests' they were imagined to bring with them and their local 'social and natural environment', should be appropriate to what were assumed to be their limited intellectual capacities, and should reveal the connection between 'life and livelihood'. The Hadow Report was, perhaps, the last to be concerned expressly with an alternative to education.

[7] Later inquiries promoted by governments (notably the Newsom Report and the Report on Higher Education, and many of the Working Papers of the Schools Council, e.g. nos. 7 and 11), while sometimes purporting to be concerned with the educational engagement, have been chiefly concerned with this substitution; that is, with the corruptions of the engagement and the extensions of the alternatives required to make them serve the current 'needs of the nation'.

to reduce or to abolish disparities of opportunity and thus to generate a 'fully integrated' society. Here, however, the design and its imposition upon the educational engagement are inseparable: the design itself requires that all schools shall be the same and that none shall be 'School'.

In pursuit of this enterprise of substitution, the chief agents, of course, have been governments; and it has been pursued in legislative proposals of various dimensions and different degrees of directness. It is a concomitant of that 'enlightened' understanding of government in which rulers are recognized as the managers of an association bent upon the achievement of some substantive 'purpose' or the enjoyment of substantial satisfactions and in which 'education' is regarded as merely a means to the chosen end. In one version of this enterprise, it is, for us, an old story. In 1821 a bill was promoted in Parliament designed to require the collegiate and grammar schools of England (with the exceptions of Eton and Westminster) to provide the sort of elementary and vocationally directed training which was being provided in the parish and charity schools and in private 'academies' and institutions of all sorts set up for the purpose. There are examples of grammar schools at that time departing from the terms of their foundation in order to engage in this activity. The other and more recent version of this enterprise, the project of replacing education with an apprenticeship to adult life governed by the consideration of 'social integration', may be illustrated in the proposals of one of its promoters. 'It is time', he writes, 'to ask more rigorously whether the present curricular differences between schools are socially divisive', and he suggests that what he calls 'the linguistic discipline' of Latin is divisive and should *on that account* be abolished. When he goes on to speculate on the 'common culture' to be disseminated in this alternative to education, his project is unmistakably the abolition of 'School': it is to be based upon 'flexible, exact and sensitive speech, creative writing, a cultivation of the living arts, an appreciation of the mass media and a concern for world affairs'.

I do not propose to follow the history or to forecast the fortunes of this design to replace education by 'socialization'. In most parts of Europe it has been a plodding engagement, enlivened by some dramatic moments and directed by the characteristic imbecility of political fanaticism. It was a project long before it became a policy; and in it those who might have devoted themselves to making the opportunity of education available to more of those who had hitherto enjoyed only an alternative to it, have devoted, themselves, instead, to its abolition. Where governments already controlled whatever there was of a genuine educational engagement, as well as the current alternative to it, the task of assimilating the one to the other has not been difficult. The outcome (as in Russia) has been a single 'system' of apprenticeship to adult life which, while it may allow considerable internal diversity, is wholly subordinate to 'social' considerations. In England, a considerable part of the educational engagement (including all the universities) has sold itself over the last fifty years to what it supposed was a benign government genuinely concerned for its survival in difficult circumstances, only to discover that it had sold itself into 'socialization' and abetted its own destruction. What remains are impoverished fragments which have to endure the threat of dissolution. Modern governments are not interested in education; they are concerned only to impose 'socialization' of one kind or another upon the surviving fragments of a once considerable educational engagement.

This situation, however, is not solely the outcome of a legislative policy bent upon denying to any what (it is supposed) some do not want or can make no use of. It would never have acquired its present dimensions had it not been promoted by contingent circumstances and abetted by intellectual confusion. The enterprise of abolishing education by substituting some version of 'socialization' has found an ally in some features of those other, concurrent, projects for the destruction of the 'School' which I have already noticed; it has been promoted, often inadvertently, by innovations in the educational engagement; it has been obscured by the noisiest of the controversies of the last fifty years (that concerned with the measurement and distribution of so-called 'intelligence'); and it has been confirmed in a corrupt way of thinking about the educational engagement itself. Something must be said about each of these self-betrayals of the engagement.

The alternative to education, invented for the poor as something instead of virtually nothing, was designed (for the most part by politicians) as an apprenticeship to adult life which, far from offering a release from the immediacies, the partialities and the abridgements of the local and contemporary world of the learner, reproduced this world in its already familiar terms and provided the learner with more information about what was already within his reach and with skills in which he was reckoned to be 'interested' because he was already aware of them in use or in his own talents. The engagement was not to initiate him into a difficult and unfamiliar inheritance of human undertakings and sentiments, but to give him a somewhat firmer grasp of what he recognized to be 'relevant' to himself as he was and to the 'facts of life'. He was not to be put in the way of understanding himself in a new context or of undergoing a palingenesis in which he acquired a more ample identity; he was merely to be provoked to see himself more clearly in the mirror of his current world. Those who promoted this alternative to education believed that its products would be 'more useful members of society'. They no more confused this apprenticeship to adult life with the educational engagement than they confused the parish with the grammar school, the *école communale* with the *lycée*, the 'public' school with the Boston Latin School, the *Realschule* with the *Gymnasium*, the 'secondary school' (in the Hadow sense) with the grammar or collegiate school, or the technical college with the university.

Nevertheless, the design of this alternative to education is both conceptually and historically connected with what purported to be a better understanding of the educational engagement itself. It was allied with the Baconian notion of 'education' as a concern with 'things, not words', as 'learning from life' and the discovery of 'how it works'; with the absence of a curriculum (each day may be relied upon to provide 'experiences' to be looked into) which might disturb the learner by suggesting unfamiliar distinctions; with the reluctance to 'foist upon children problems which do not develop from their own interests' and with the desired and foreseen abolition of 'School' which comes from the dissolution of the difference between 'School' and the local world. In short, the political project of *substituting* 'socialization' for education has been sustained by beliefs about the educational engagement itself in which the alternative appeared, not as a valuable but admittedly inferior article, designed originally for the poor, but as an *educationally* superior article. Without this support (spurious though it is) this enterprise of substitution would, no doubt, have been more difficult.

These beliefs made little impact upon the educational engagement of Europe; they were hostile, not to the contingent vices of schools, but to the virtues embedded in the idea 'School'. The engagement (represented in the *Gymnasium*, the *lycée*, the grammar and collegiate schools and elsewhere) had educational traditions capable of resisting the enterprise of destroying it by assimilating it to the alternative. But in recent times there have been changes in curriculum and in methods of teaching which, sometimes inadvertently, have pushed the engagement in the direction of the alternative by allowing 'social' considerations in some measure to oust educational ones. The emergence of 'science' in the curriculum of schools and the study of languages are two examples out of many of this self-corruption of the educational engagement.

87

If 'science' had entered the educational engagement as an initiation into an intellectual adventure recognized as a component of an inheritance of human understandings and beliefs it would, no doubt, have constituted a benign and an appropriate addition to what was already there. But it did not. 'Science' belonged, instead and in the first place, to the alternative for education, designed to 'socialize', where it was recognized as useful information about the world related to some skill, craft or fabricating activity – what the Hadow Report was later to call 'practical science'; and when, thus understood, it was allowed to graduate to compose part of an educational engagement it was clearly eccentric to the engagement. Becoming established in this naïve Baconian idiom as an alleged knowledge of 'things' not words, of objects not ideas, of observations not thoughts, as the Rousseauistic *leçon des choses* which still appears in the *lycée* programme, it was confirmed in its eccentricity: its intellectual despicability could not be concealed.

Nevertheless, 'science' did find a place for itself in 'School'. It was, with some difficulty, detached from immediate vocational considerations; it remained for a long time 'useful information' about the natural world with which every educated man should be acquainted,[8] but in the course of time (within living memory) something has been done to give it recognition as one of the great intellectual pursuits of mankind: but without notable success. It is now taught and learned more seriously, but its place in current educational arrangements remains ambiguous: chemistry, for example, has never outgrown its character as a sophisticated kind of cookery, and 'science' is still defended in terms of 'social', not educational, considerations: 'We *need* first-class surgeons, engineers, chemists, psychologists, social scientists, etc.', and unless they are started on their way in school we shall not get what our hope of affluence requires for its fulfilment.

Flattered by circumstance and linked with ancient heresy, an attempt was made to promote 'science' itself as a 'culture' in which human beings identified themselves in relation to 'things' and to their 'empire over things',[9] but it now deceives nobody; boys do not elect for the 'science sixth' expecting to achieve self-knowledge, but for vocational reasons. Regrettably, this is not yet the case

[8] When Thomas Huxley regretted the absence of 'science' from the school curriculum, what he regretted was the absence of the opportunity for a learner to acquire an 'outfit drawn from the stores of physical science', 'a knowledge of what physcial science has done in the last century'.

[9] Renan opposed 'positive science' to the 'superficial humanism' of school education and recognized it as a moral culture.

with the no less fraudulent claims of the so-called 'social sciences' which have been pushed into the curriculum of schools and universities, but the reckoning cannot be far off. For a generation now they have remained in business only on account of their technological pretensions.

The educational engagement in respect of languages is to initiate learners into a language as a source and a repository of human understandings and sentiments, and it was this which the collegiate and grammar schools of England and their equivalents elsewhere undertook in respect of Latin and Greek and, to a lesser extent, in respect of a native language. What the learner submitted himself to was not a 'linguistic discipline' but an initiation into exactitudes of thought and generosities of feeling, into literatures and into histories in which the 'fact of life' was illuminated by a 'quality of life'. When modern languages became part of our educational engagement (first, perhaps, in schools for girls) they were chosen for their literatures and they were designed to provoke the learner to identify himself in terms of a larger European culture: it was to read Lessing and Goethe, Molière and Racine, Dante and Leopardi, Cervantes and Calderón.

The counterpart to this in the alternative for education was, however, a different kind of undertaking, dominated by the belief that 'language is but the instrument conveying to us things useful to be known'. The languages taught were chosen in respect of 'social' (that is, commercial or local), not educational, considerations; and they were learnt merely as a means of communication. It was this extrinsic 'purpose' which made appropriate the methods of learning from which have emerged audio-visual language machines, 'language laboratories' and 'language laboratory assistants' instead of persons who had a profound knowledge of the languages, the literatures and the histories concerned. The alleged virtue of language machines is that 'they teach people to speak languages with confidence, and they do it fast', a virtue appropriate to the enterprise; and no harm would have been done if what was appropriate to the alternative to education, both in choice of languages and in methods of learning, had not been taken into the educational engagement and corrupted it. When it is said that a child should learn a foreign language as he learns his native language, 'by hearing it spoken', what is being overlooked is that in the educational engagement of 'School' what he learns of his native language is precisely what never could be learned by 'hearing it spoken'.

The self-corruption of universities exceeds that of any other part of the educational engagement of European peoples. In times past English universities have often been indolent guardians of the engagement to educate and as often they have recovered, but for a generation now they have anticipated almost every design of governments to transform them into instruments of 'socialization', hardly needing to be bribed to undertake this destruction of themselves. Nevertheless they have, of course, received a considerable push in this direction, not least in the Report of the Committee on Higher Education (1963), which assimilates them into a system of so-called 'higher education', understood as an investment in learners who have acquired certain qualifications, designed to equip them with the specially complicated skills and versatilities increasingly required if the nation is to satisfy 'the aims of economic growth' and 'to compete successfully with other highly developed countries in an era of rapid technological and social advance'. No doubt universities are intended by the Committee to have a place of their own in this 'higher education', but they are to submit to the extrinsic purpose, the 'social' considerations, which identify it as an alternative to education. In the event, the disaster is not that they are being swamped by persons in search of almost anything but education, but their almost total destruction as an educational engagement.

The design to substitute 'socialization' for education has gone far enough to be recognized as the most momentous occurrence of this century, the greatest of the adversities to have overtaken our culture, the beginning of a dark age devoted to barbaric affluence. It emerged from a project, embarked upon about three centuries ago (which was neither stupid nor itself menacing to the educational engagement) to provide an alternative to education for those who, for whatever reason, fell outside the educational engagement. Since those times this alternative has been adjusted to respond to changing circumstance; it has been improved and extended to compose an apprenticeship to adult domestic, industrial and commercial life, it has generated a variety of versions of itself, and for the most part it has submitted to the direction of governments. Indeed, it has become what the world it has helped to create can recognize as a 'service industry'. It was designed as a contribution to the well-being of 'the nation'; it has been welcomed or endured on account of the affluence it is alleged to be about to procure, and attempts have been made to calculate its product in terms of costs and benefits; and it has been defended on the ground of what it is designed to produce and upon the more questionable plea that it is the most appropriate apprenticeship for certain sorts of children.

This makeshift for education, however, was permitted to corrupt the educational engagement of European peoples, and it is now proclaimed as its desirable successor. The usurpation has everywhere been set on foot.

But the victim of this enterprise is not merely an historic educational engagement (with all its faults and shortcomings); it is also the idea of education as an initiation into an inheritance of human understandings in virtue of which a man might be released from the 'fact of life' and recognize himself in terms of a 'quality of life'. The calamity of the enterprise is matched by the intellectual corruption of the enterprisers.

There were, in the past, naïve promoters of the most common version of this enterprise who believed it to be unfortunate that there should be schools not expressly designed to impart to learners information about the world they were about to enter and in fact often failing to impart this information in sufficient quantity because of their concern with an inheritance of human understandings; but they did not deny that such schools existed. Like Bacon they recognized Westminster College and probably recognized it to have some virtue, but they preferred Gresham College; and even Mr. E. Robinson recognized the existence of what he calls 'academic' education, although he deplores it as a grossly imperfect apprenticeship to adult life when compared with the excitement offered by 'the new polytechnics'.

There are others who do not deny the difference but who mistake the distinction; while intending to defend the educational engagement against one version of 'socialization' they use arguments which merely identify it with another, and in this manner, inadvertently perhaps, banish education from the scence. For example, there are writers who are opposed to that version of 'socialization' in which the considerations which govern the apprenticeship to adult life are an overriding concern for 'social integration'. But the reason they give for their opposition is not that the project is destructive of the educational engagement, but only that its outcome will almost certainly be a lowering of the standards of achievement and a consequent failure to satisfy the need of society for a constant supply of first-class engineers, doctors, economists, teachers, mathematicians, chemists, technicians, and so on. So far as anyone can foresee, their expectations are likely to be fulfilled; at all events, these writers are correct in recognizing what they oppose as a calculated indifference to scholastic achievement and an earnest desire to impose a *solidarité de sottise*. But to oppose it on the grounds that it will hinder the appearance of 'a succession of adults who possess the advanced skills upon which our survival depends' is to have surrendered to the false doctrine that education is to be understood as an investment of the human resources of the nation in an attempt not to be outdistanced in affluence by America, Russia or Japan. In short, these writers recognize a difference between education and its alternatives, but mistake the distinction as one of the standards of achievement in the pursuit of an extrinsic 'purpose'.

But the determined promoters of the enterprise to destroy education are restrained by no such lingering recognition of an educational engagement. They represent themselves as persons who have perceived a 'truth' which prejudice has concealed from others; namely, that everything has a 'social function', that everything is what its 'social function' declares it to be, and that, consequently there never were and never could be educational as distinct from 'social' considerations in respect of the apprenticeship of newcomers to an adult human life. Thus, it is said that 'the function of the public school and university system [sic] has been to train a ruling élite, that 'the public school was developed to run an empire', that 'the ancient universities of Europe were founded to promote the training of the clergy, doctors and lawyers', that the function of a modern university is to impart 'skills which demand special training' and that most undergraduates know this to be the case and go there to acquire such skills, and so on.[10] It is said, in short, that education has never been anything other than a 'social investment' related (often imperfectly) to 'the needs of a society in respect of instruction'. Consequently (they continue), intelligent reflection about education must be reflection about the appropriateness of a current educational engagement to the needs of a current society; and educational reform (when it is not concerned merely with methods of teaching and learning) is detecting what are the 'functions' which together constitute a current society and devising a 'system of education' which will produce most economically the most adequate performers of these functions. When these projectors settle upon 'economic development', 'the fight for economic survival' or 'keeping up in the economic race' as the engagement to be provided for, and represent themselves as the designers

[10] In the confusion of para. 25 of the Report of the Committee on Higher Education it is allowed that a few undergraduates may go to a university for the marginally different extrinsic purpose of acquiring 'pure knowledge' (which also has to be found a 'social function' in order to become visible); but no one is credited with going for no extrinsic purpose at all but merely to continue his education, because the possibility of any such activity as being educated is ruled out in advance.

of an apprenticeship to adult life in which every child learns to identify himself as a (perhaps functionally distinguished) member of a development corporation, they have no difficulty in appearing as benign reformers, doing no more than releasing the educational engagement from antiquated 'social' considerations and bringing it up to date. The fact that their design for 'education' corresponds (with, of course, the appropriate enlargements) to the alternative for education devised in the seventeenth century for the poor is regarded as a tribute to the genius of the inventors of that alternative, who may be criticized only for not at once setting about the destruction of schools and universities which were, even then, providing performers for functions of declining significance. Thus, the destruction of an educational engagement proceeds behind a veil of conceptual nonsense and historical rubbish, now called 'the sociology of education', and designed to persuade us that what is being destroyed never existed.

Education, I have contended, is the transaction between the generations in which newcomers to the scene are initiated into the world which they are to inhabit. This is a world of understandings, imaginings, meanings, moral and religious beliefs, relationships, practices – states of mind in which the human condition is to be discerned as recognitions of and responses to the ordeal of consciousness. These states of mind can be entered into only by being themselves understood, and they can be understood only by learning to do so. To be initiated into this world is learning to become human; and to move within it freely is being human, which is an 'historic', not a 'natural' condition.

Thus, an educational engagement is at once a discipline and a release; and it is the one by virtue of being the other. It is a difficult engagement of learning by study in a continuous and exacting redirection of attention and refinement of understanding which calls for humility, patience and courage. Its reward is an emancipation from the mere 'fact of living', from the immediate contingencies of place and time of birth, from the tyranny of the moment and from the servitude of a merely current condition; it is the reward of a human identity and of a character capable in some measure of the moral and intellectual adventure which constitutes a specifically human life.

Consequently, education is not be confused with that accommodation to circumstances in which a newcomer learns the latest steps in the *danse macabre* of wants and satisfactions and thus acquires a 'current' value in the world. Some of these steps, the 'specially complicated skills and versatilities' of which the Report on

Higher Education speaks, have become intricate, and to learn them is an exacting task. But nothing a man may learn in this respect has anything whatsoever to do with education.

It is now about two centuries since our educational engagement began to be corrupted by having imposed upon it the character of a school of dancing. This usurpation has been promoted by confused beliefs about the transaction itself, and it has been procured by 'enlightened' governments. It is now far advanced. Fragments of an educational engagement, however, remain: relatively uncorrupt schools, universities which have not entirely surrendered the character of educational institutions, and teachers who refuse to become dancing-masters. Moreover, with some at least, the urge to destroy 'School' by depriving it of its character of a serious engagement to learn by study may, perhaps, be interpreted as a misdirected attempt to escape the enormities of 'socialization': when to teach is identified with 'socialization', education becomes the engagement to teach nothing. Caught between these destructive winds of obliquely opposed doctrine our engagement to educate is torn asunder.

THE IDEA OF A UNIVERSITY

1950

It is a favourite theory of mine that what people call 'ideals' and 'purposes' are never themselves the source of human activity; they are shorthand expressions for the real spring of conduct, which is a disposition to do certain things and a knowledge of how to do them. Human beings do not start from rest and spring into activity only when attracted by a purpose to be achieved. To be alive is to be perpetually active. The purposes we attribute to particular kinds of activity are only abridgements of our knowledge of how to engage in this or that activity.

This, for example, is obviously so in the activity we call 'science'. Scientific activity is not the pursuit of a premeditated end; nobody knows or can imagine where it will reach. There is no perfection, prefigured in our minds, which we can set up as a standard by which to judge current achievements. What holds science together and gives it impetus and direction is not a known purpose to be achieved, but the knowledge scientists have of how to conduct a scientific investigation. Their particular pursuits and purposes are not superimposed upon that knowledge, but emerge within it. Or again, a cook is not a man who first has the vision of a pie and then tries to make it; he is a man skilled in cookery, and both his projects and his achievements spring from his skill. Or, to take a

Editorial note: This piece, first published in *The Listener*, is in part a distillation of 'The Universities' (pp. 127–8). However, it contains some new material and provides a succinct introduction to Oakeshott's thought on the subject, and is therefore reproduced here in its entirety.

third example, a man may think he has a 'mission' in life, and he may think that his activity is governed by this 'mission'. But, in fact, it is the other way about; his missionary activity consists in knowing how to behave in a certain way and in trying to behave in that way; and what he calls his 'mission' is only a shorthand expression of this knowledge and endeavour.

For this reason, the current talk about the 'mission' and the 'function' of a university goes rather over my head; I think I can understand what is intended, but it seems to me an unfortunate way of talking. It assumes that there is something called 'a university', a contrivance of some sort, something you could make another of tomorrow if you had enough money, of which it it sensible to ask, What is it 'for'? And one of the criticisms of contemporary universities is that they are not as clear as they ought to be about their 'function'. I am not at all surprised. There is plenty that might properly be criticized in our universities, but to quarrel with them because they are not clear about their 'function' is to make a mistake about their character. A university is not a machine for achieving a particular purpose or producing a particular result; it is a manner of human activity. And it would be necessary for a university to advertise itself as pursuing a particular purpose only if it were talking to people so ignorant that they had to be spoken to in baby-language, or if it were so little confident of its power to embrace those who came to it that it had to call attention to its incidental charms. My impression, however, is that our universities have not yet sunk so low as to make this necessary. They may not know what they are 'for', they may be very hazy about their 'function', but I think they do know something that is much more important – namely, how to go about the business of being a university. This knowledge is not a gift of nature; it is a knowledge of a tradition, it has to be acquired, it is always mixed up with error and ignorance, and it may even be lost. But, it is only by exploring this sort of knowledge (which I believe not to have been lost) that we can hope to discover what may be called the 'idea' of a university.

A university is a number of people engaged in a certain sort of activity: the Middle Ages called it *Studium*; we may call it 'the pursuit of learning'. This activity is one of the properties, indeed one of the virtues, of a civilized way of living; the scholar has his place beside the poet, the priest, the soldier, the politician and the man of business in any civilized society. The universities do not, however, have a monopoly of this activity. The hermit scholar in his study, an academy famous for a particular branch of learning, a school for young children, are each participants in this activity and each of them is admirable, but they are not universities. What distinguishes a university is a special manner of engaging in the pursuit of learning. It is a corporate body of scholars, each devoted to a particular branch of learning: what is characteristic is the pursuit of learning as a co-operative enterprise. The members of this corporation are not spread about the world, meeting occasionally or not at all; they live in permanent proximity to one another. And consequently we should neglect part of the character of a university if we omitted to think of it as a place. A university, moreover, is a home of learning, a place where a tradition of learning is preserved and extended, and where the necessary apparatus for the pursuit of learning has been gathered together.

Of the scholars who compose a university, some may be expected to devote an unbroken leisure to learning, their fellows having the advantage of their knowledge from their conversation and the world benefiting, perhaps, from their writings. A place of learning without this kind of scholar could scarcely be called a university. Others, however, will engage themselves to teach as well as to learn. But here again, it is the special manner of the pedagogic enterprise which distinguishes a university. Those who come to be taught at a university have to provide evidence that they are not merely beginners; and not only do they have displayed before them the learning of their teachers, but they are offered a curriculum of study, to be followed by a test and the award of a degree. Three classes of person, then, go to compose a university as we know it – the scholar, the scholar who is also a teacher, and those who come to be taught, the undergraduates. And the presence of these three classes, and the relations that prevail between them, determine the distinctive place of a university in the wider enterprise we call the pursuit of learning.

Let us consider the activity of these three classes. Everyone who knows anything about it, knows that there is a difference between the pursuit of learning and the acquisition of information. It is a subtle difference, for an ill-informed man can scarcely be called a learned man. But a scholar is something more than a picker-up of unconsidered trifles: he knows something about what he is looking for, and he can distinguish between what he knows and what he does not know. The world's contempt for the 'poor pedant' is often mistaken; it judges the scholar's activity by its use, and finds it pedantic when it appears useless. But this is a false standard; what is reprehensible is not the pursuit of knowledge which has no immediate use, nor that attention to detail which is unavoidable in scholarship, but that blind groping about among fragments of learning which are known only as fragments into which scholarship sometimes degenerates. This does not happen as often as the world thinks; and perhaps it is less liable to happen in a university than elsewhere.

There is, indeed, no simple way of determining what composes the world of learning; no clear reason – such as usefulness – can be found to justify its parts. They do not represent a premeditated purpose, but a slowly changing tradition. As the years pass, new studies rise above the horizon and old studies are rejuvenated by coming in contact with the new. Unavoidably, each scholar is something of a specialist who cultivates a chosen field. But it rarely happens that this is a very narrow field, and a scholar may often be found turning from one study to another or poking his nose into something which is not his chief business. Nevertheless, the pursuit of learning may have the appearance of a fragmentary enterprise; and even if we suspect that this is what it looks like when seen only from the outside, it will not seem far-fetched to enquire whether some superior integrating force is not wanted to give coherence and proportion to the whole pursuit. Do we not need a map, it may plausibly be asked, a map on which the relations between the parts of the world of learning are clearly displayed? Would not the whole thing be better for a little glue to hold it together? And some who feel most strongly about this are to be found filling in the interstices between the sciences with a sticky mess called 'culture', in the belief that they are supplying a desperate need. But both the diagnosis and the remedy spring from a sad misconception.

The world of learning needs no extraneous cement to hold it together; its parts move in a single magnetic field, and the need for go-betweens arises only when the current is gratuitously cut off. The pursuit of learning is not a race in which the competitors jockey for the best place, it is not even an argument or a symposium; it is a conversation. And the peculiar virtue of a university (as a place of many studies) is to exhibit it in this character, each study appearing as a voice whose tone is neither tyrannous nor plangent, but humble and conversable. A conversation does not need a chairman, it has no predetermined course, we do not ask what it is 'for', and we do not judge its excellence by its conclusion; it has no conclusion, but is always put by for another day. Its integration is not superimposed but springs from the quality of the voices which speak, and its value lies in the relics it leaves behind in the minds of those who participate.

The scholar, then, is one who knows how to engage in the activity of learning; his natural voice is not that of the preacher or of the instructor. Yet it is not surprising that among scholars should be found teachers, and that university should be a place where one might go with the expectation of learning something. Not every scholar will have the sympathy that makes a great teacher, but every genuine scholar unavoidably imparts to those capable of recognizing it something of his knowledge on how to pursue learning. His power to teach springs from the force and inspiration of his knowledge, from his immersion in the pursuit of learning, which may be felt even by those little touched with the ambitions of a scholar. And even those whose learning and sympathy are ready, those who are pre-eminently capable of imparting what they know, must be expected to be something different from assiduous instructors. They may be trusted to know the rules, but they will not be much concerned to teach conclusions. One may go to some sorts of art schools and be taught ten ways of drawing a cat of a dozen tricks to remember in painting an eye, but the scholar as teacher will teach, not how to draw or to paint, but how to see. He may be easily articulate, or he may find it difficult to throw off his own doubts and hesitancies, but, since he is a scholar, it does not belong to his character to speak with no voice in particular, and he will have nothing to do with vulgarization of learning which regards it merely as a means to passing an examination or winning a certificate.

But a university may be credited with a power to teach which goes beyond that of its individual scholars. It is not an academy drawing its inspiration from a single pre-eminent man; it is a body of scholars who supply one another's imperfections, both personal and scholastic. It accommodates many different sorts of teacher, and each sort draws its power from its intercourse with other sorts. When we commend the easily articulate don who has a ready answer for all our questions, we should remember that he is not simply a superlatively lively mind but is often the spokesman for the less articulate and perhaps more profound and original minds with which he is in daily communication: without them he would hardly exist. A university, then, is an institution peculiarly well-adapted to the weakness and ignorance of mankind because its excellence does not depend upon the appearance of a universal genius, though it knows how to make room for one should one emerge. Moreover, like the House of Commons or an old established business, it imparts something without having expressly to teach it; and what it imparts in this way is at least the manners of the conversation.

The scholar, the teacher, and lastly those who come to be taught, the undergraduate: he, or she, also has a distinctive character. First, he is not a child, not a beginner. He has already had his schooling elsewhere, and has learned enough, morally and intellectually, to take a chance with himself upon the open sea. He is neither a child nor an adult, but stands in a strange middle moment of life when he knows only enough of himself and of the world which passes before him to wish to know more. He has not yet found what he loves, but neither is he jealous of time, of accidents, or of rivals. Perhaps the phrase from the fairy tale suits him best – he has come to seek his intellectual fortune. But, further, he is not the first who has passed from school to university, he is not like a stranger who knows nothing of what to expect, so that everything has to be explained to him on his arrival in words of one syllable. And if the tradition to which he belongs has already taught him anything, it will have taught him that he will not find his intellectual fortune, once and for all, in three years at a university. He is, therefore, we may suppose, in tune with what he is to find and is prepared to make use of it.

And what does he find? If he is not unlucky, he finds a strongly flowing current of activity, men and women engaged in the pursuit of learning, and an invitation to participate in some manner in this activity. This invitation is extended alike to those already touched by an ambition for a life of learning and to those who have no such ambition. A university is not a contrivance for making scholars; its ideal is not a world populated solely by scholars. For about 400 years in England the education of the would-be scholar and of the man of the world has been the same, and this tradition belongs to our idea of a university.

Beyond this, a university would be found to offer the undergraduate a limited variety of studies from which to make his choice; for, of course, it is discriminating about what it teaches, and not everything that engages the attentions of its scholars is thought suitable for undergraduate study. Where this particular selection of subjects came from, it would be hard to say. Some are old, others new; some – like medicine and law – have a semi-professional appearance, others have little direct connection with the world outside. Certainly none of these studies owes its place in a university curriculum to any reason so simple as its professional usefulness or because the knowledge concerned is easy to teach or easy to test. Indeed, the only characteristic common to them all is that of being a recognized branch of scholarship; in each the pursuit of learning is reflected and consequently each has within itself

– when we drink deeply of it – a power to educate. Together they represent, at least in outline, the conversation which is being carried on in the university; and the undergraduate would never be tempted to mistake his university for an institute in which only one voice was heard, or for a polytechnic in which only the mannerisms of the voices were taught.

This, then, to the undergraduate, is the distinctive mark of a university; it is a place where he has the opportunity of education in conversation with his teachers, his fellows and himself, and where he is not encouraged to confuse education with training for a profession, with learning the tricks of a trade, with preparation for future particular service in society or with the acquisition of a kind of moral and intellectual outfit to see him through life. Whenever an ulterior purpose of this sort makes its appearance, education (which is concerned with persons, not functions) steals out of the back door with noiseless steps. The pursuit of learning for the power it may bring has its roots in a covetous egoism which is not less egoistic or less covetous when it appears as a so-called 'social purpose', and with this a university has nothing to do. The form of its curriculum has no such design; and the manner of its teaching – teachers interested in the pupil himself, in what he is thinking, in the quality of his mind, in his immortal soul, and not in what sort of a schoolmaster or administrator he can be made into – the manner of this teaching has no such intention.

But further, a university has something else to offer the undergraduate, and I take this to be its most characteristic gift because it is exclusive to a university and is rooted in the character of university education as neither a beginning nor an end, but a middle. A man may at any time in his life begin to explore a new branch of learning or engage in fresh activity, but only at a university may he do this without a rearrangement of his scarce resources of time and energy; in later life he is committed to so much that he cannot easily throw off. The characteristic gift of a university is the gift of an interval. Here is an opportunity to put aside the hot allegiances of youth without the necessity of at once acquiring new loyalties to take their place. Here is a break in the tyrannical course of irreparable events; a period in which to look round upon the world and upon oneself without the sense of an enemy at one's back or the insistent pressure to make up one's mind; a moment in which to taste the mystery without the necessity of at once seeking a solution. And all this, not in an intellectual vacuum, but surrounded by all the inherited learning and literature and experience of our civilization; not alone, but in the company of kindred spirits;

not as a sole occupation, but combined with the discipline of studying a recognized branch of learning; and neither as a first step in
education (for those wholly ignorant of how to behave or think) nor
as a final education to fit a man for the day of judgement, but as a
middle. This interval is nothing so commonplace as a pause to get
one's breath; no young man or woman, I take it, would say 'Thank
you' for an opportunity of that sort; it is not the cessation of
activity, but the occasion of a unique kind of activity.

It would be difficult to determine the generation of this remarkable opportunity. Perhaps it sprang (as Lucretius imagines human
limbs to have sprung) from there being people who, in varying
degrees, could make use of it. At all events, I think it is the one
thing that every university in Europe, in some measure, provides
for its undergraduates. The enjoyment of it depends upon some
previous preparation (no man ignorant of what he should have
learned in the nursery could expect to make use of it), but it does
not depend on any definable pre-existing privilege or upon the
absence of the necessity of earning one's living in the end – it is
itself the privilege of being a 'student', the enjoyment of *schole* –
leisure. One might, hazarding a misunderstanding, reduce this to a
doctrine about the character of a university; one might call it the
doctrine of the interim. But the doctrine would be no more than a
brief expression of what it felt like to be an undergraduate on that
first October morning. Almost overnight, a world of ungracious
fact had melted into infinite possibility; we who belonged to no
'leisured class' had been freed for a moment from the curse of
Adam, the burdensome distinction between work and play. What
opened before us was not a road but a boundless sea; it was enough
to stretch one's sails to the wind. The distracting urgency of an
immediate destination was absent, duty no longer oppressed,
boredom and disappointment were words without meaning; death
was unthinkable. But it belongs to the character of an interim to
come to an end; there is a time for everything and nothing should
be prolonged beyond its time. The eternal undergraduate is a lost
soul.

And what of the harvest? Nobody could go down from such a
university unmarked. Intellectually, he may be supposed to have
acquired some knowledge, and, more important, a certain discipline
of mind, a grasp of consequences, a greater command over his own
powers. He will know, perhaps, that it is not good enough to have a
'point of view', that what we need is *thoughts*. He will not go down
in possession of an armoury of arguments to prove the truth of
what he believes; but he will have acquired something that puts

him beyond the reach of the intellectual hooligan, and whatever has been the subject of his study he may be expected to be able to look for some meaning in the things that have greatly moved mankind. Perhaps he may even have found a centre for his intellectual affections. In short, this period at a university may not have equipped him very effectively to earn a living, but he will have learned something to help him lead a more significant life. And morally – he will not have acquired an outfit of moral ideas, a new reach-me-down suit of moral clothing, but he will have had an opportunity to extend the range of his moral sensibility, and he will have had the leisure to replace the clamorous and conflicting absolutes of adolescence with something less corruptible.

The pursuit of learning, like every other great activity, is unavoidably conservative. A university is not like a dinghy which can be jiggled about to catch every transient breath of wind. The critics it should listen to are those who are interested in the pursuit of learning, not those who find a university imperfect because it is not something other than it is. But somehow or other the idea of a university in recent years has got mixed up with notions such as 'higher education', 'advanced training', refresher courses for adults' – things admirable in themselves, but really very little to do with a university. And it is time something was done to unravel the confusion. For these ideas belong to a world of power and utility, of exploitation, of social and individual egoism, and of activity, whose meaning lies outside itself in some trivial result or achievement – and this is not the world to which a university belongs; it is not the world to which education in the true sense belongs. It is a very powerful world; it is wealthy, interfering and well-meaning. But it is not remarkably self-critical; it is apt to mistake itself for the whole world, and with amiable carelessness it assumes that whatever does not contribute to its own purposes is somehow errant. A university needs to beware of the patronage of this world, or it will find that it has sold its birthright for a mess of pottage; it will find that instead of studying and teaching the languages and literatures of the world it has become a school for training interpreters, that instead of pursuing science it is engaged in training electrical engineers or industrial chemists, that instead of studying history it is studying and teaching history for some ulterior purpose, that instead of educating men and women it is training them exactly to fill some niche in society.

A university, like everything else, has a place in the society to which it belongs, but that place is not the function of contributing to some other kind of activity in the society but of being itself and not another thing. Its first business is with the pursuit of learning – there is no substitute which, in a university, will make up for the absence of this – and, secondly, its concern is with the sort of education that has been found to spring up in the course of this activity. A university will have ceased to exist when its learning has degenerated into what is now called research, when its teaching has become mere instruction and occupies the whole of an undergraduate's time, and when those who came to be taught come, not in search of their intellectual fortune but with a vitality so unroused or so exhausted that they wish only to be provided with a serviceable moral and intellectual outfit; when they come with no understanding of the manners of conversation but desire only a qualification for earning a living or a certificate to let them in on the exploitation of the world.

THE UNIVERSITIES

1949

Critics of the universities have appeared in every generation. The criticism has come from within and from without; from teachers, from the taught and from the great and often ignorant world. It has ranged from malicious detraction to the quiet consideration of manifest defects which has been the source of all fruitful reform. And it has concerned itself with every level of the life of the universities. The book before me,[1] the latest addition to this library of criticism, is the result of a communal enterprise: a group of like-minded men and women (a self-appointed working-party), at meetings spread over the last two years, has considered what before then had been recognized as the critical situation of the universities, and Sir Walter Moberly has attempted to 'crystallize the interim results' of these discussions. The group has found a spokesman who has most of the necessary qualifications; his knowledge of British universities is great and spread over a long period, his mind is vigorous and he conforms to Thomas Arnold's dictum that 'no one ought to meddle with the universities, who does not know them well and love them well'. His is by no means an indulgent love, and there are moments when he seems to go out of his way to display an erratic and ill-considered severity. But the result is a book which deserves to be studied.

The critic, however, calls forth criticism. Only a blind and trivial loyalty would resent Sir Walter's diagnosis of the shortcomings of

[1] Sir Walter Moberly, *The Crisis in the Universities* (London: SCM Prss, 1949).

British universities at the present time, only an unnatural fixity of mind would find nothing to reflect profitably upon in his suggestions for improvement, and one would have to be very insensitive to remain untouched by the tone in which the book is written. Yet in each of these respects something remains to be said; and if it is said clearly and with as little beating about the bush as may be, it will perhaps be recognized as a contribution to the discussion and not mistaken for an alien and unfriendly voice. But first a limitation must be observed. The book is 'written from a Christian standpoint', but it is no part of my project to investigate this standpoint, except to say that the particular form of Christianity which appears here is not everybody's Christianity; indeed, it seems to me exceedingly eccentric. And it is possible to say something relevant about the book without considering its standpoint, because much of what it has to say is independent of its Christian predisposition. This does not mean that the Christianity of the book is merely peripheral to its argument; indeed it is made clear that, in the mind of the writer, both the diagnosis of the crisis and the suggestions for reform and certainly the tone of the book, spring from Christian conviction. But it is recognized that something more precise and detailed is needed than an exhortation to become Christian, and, courageously, 'back to the Christian tradition' is placed among the spurious remedies of the crisis.

Briefly, the argument of the book is as follows. We are living in an age of exceptional crisis; our condition is one of extreme physical, emotional and intellectual insecurity. As the result of a long history of discovery and invention we are already possessed of immense power, and the process which gave us this power continues unabated. This power, unavoidably, is in the hands of the few; 'a decision in the Kremlin or the White House may revolutionize the lives of millions'. Some people, intoxicated by the sense of power, see in this situation an opportunity which, if it can be exploited, may lead to the conquest of even death itself. But the power is already so great that it is felt by the ordinary man to have itself taken charge of his life, and consequently his dominant experience is one of hopeless physical insecurity. At the same time, and springing partly from the same cause, our world-picture has been shattered, we have lost our sense of direction and in our uncertainty we have become emotionally and intellectually 'displaced persons'. 'The beliefs which govern men's actions are in flux.' This is the greatest of the recent changes that have come over the world in which we live, but it is not the only one. The other significant change is that which is indicated by the word 'democracy', which among its multifarious implications involves the disappearance of anything in the nature of a ruling class: any man may find himself among those who control the available power.

In the past, the universities in this and other European countries have usually reflected the world in which they have found themselves, and they have often provided for some of the needs of that world. The universities which Newman and Paulsen described, the one exemplifying the then current Christian-Hellenic tradition and the other the tradition of liberal education, were each adapted to their worlds. Consequently we ought to consider what, if anything, the universities of contemporary Britain are doing 'to adapt themselves to a world of insecurity'. In some respects our universities reflect the changes that have already taken place, though the relics of adaptations to conditions now past distort and qualify this reflection. But when we ask, further, if our universities are providing anything to assuage the crisis of our time, the answer is that they are doing nothing. Virtually no attempt is made to provide the mental and spiritual security which the undergraduate needs and desires. Not only is he given no 'answer' to his questions, but he is not even incited to find an 'answer' for himself. 'Most students go through our universities without ever having been forced to exercise their minds on the issues which are really fundamental.' 'Owing to the prevailing fragmentation of studies' the minds of undergraduates receive no encouragement to achieve an integrated view of the world: the university has become a polytechnic. And the fragments are presented in a way that 'shirks the fundamental issues', with the consequences that the undergraduate remains as 'uneducated' as his teachers but, being younger, is less complacent about it. This dismal failure is the 'crisis in the university'.

The current remedies for this situation are found on investigation to be spurious. A return either to the tradition of 'classical humanism' or to the Christian tradition as it was in the past, is impossible; and even if either of these traditions were successfully revived, it would leave the universities out of touch with the contemporary world. 'Classical humanism' is 'bound up with a society based upon privilege' and is 'deficient in catholicity since it has little room for natural science and underrates its significance'; and a university enclosed within 'a Christian institutional framework would be so divorced from the opinions of the majority, that it could only be set up by force or by dexterous diplomacy.' And the remedy suggested by what is called 'scientific humanism' (the view that the world's chief need today is further technical advance and that the sought-after integration is to be found in this enterprise which itself requires no custodian), while it deserves serious consideration, is incomplete and less plausible than it was ten years ago. To overcome the crisis, therefore, nothing short of a revolutionary change is necessary, a 'drastic Metanoia'. The whole aim and basis of the university must be investigated; its curriculum of studies, its methods of teaching, its way of life and its relationship to society must be reconsidered if the 'deep-seated disabilities' from which it now suffers are to be removed. The task is of the greatest urgency; the sands are running out.

2

The major premiss of this argument is the alleged critical character of the times in which we live: 'for the history of civilization, the years round 1950 are critical in a degree to which the years round 1850 or 1900 were not'. We must, then, consider first the interpretation of the crisis which is set before us. Two world-wars, the invention of the atomic bomb and the presumed existence of a will to use it, have brought us to the edge of an abyss – so the diagnosis runs. We are in the situation of the inhabitants of Herculaneum and Pompeii in the summer of the year 79 AD. And our activity is not crippled by the apprehension of impending disaster only because 'our imaginations have not kept pace with our reason'. The young, however, are less deluded: there is a whole generation which has not got the normal expectation of life – and knows it. 'Many a student's life is dominated by *Angst*.'

Now, this is an unfortunate start for the diagnosis; what is merely incidental – indeed, what is trivial – gets all the emphasis. The degree of physical security one needs is very much what one is accustomed to, and we are getting accustomed to very much less than was normal fifty years ago. In spite of its sensitiveness to what the young are thinking, this book springs from a mind which is accustomed to a far greater degree of security than the young know anything about. And further, intellectual and spiritual stability is not a mere function of physical and social security; indeed, it often happens that the kind of self-questioning which shakes a man to his foundations has a background of quite undisturbed physical and social security. No man has ever been more worried about himself than Matthew Arnold in 1849, but few enjoyed greater 'security' than he did at that time. The fact is that nobody with firm beliefs is going to lose any sleep on account of a diminution of his expectation of life, and nothing is less relevant to the firmness of his beliefs than the mere length of a man's life. The shadow of the atomic bomb here obscures the diagnosis.

But there is something more in Sir Walter's mind, something of which the bomb is only a symbol. 'The sensational triumph of applied science in the last two or three centuries, bringing with it a quite new power of transforming the conditions of life, is one of the great turning-points of history': we possess immense power but lack discrimination in its use. And the crisis here is the absence of discrimination and the consequent feeling of being controlled by something we have created. The threat is not merely to individual existence, but to what we call 'civilization'. And the suggestion is that 'civilization can be saved only by a moral and intellectual and spiritual revolution to match the scientific, technological and economic revolution in which we are now living'.

But even on this wider view, the reading of the situation is, I think, at once too alarmist and too optimistic. The tone of this book is one of desperate urgency; it has the hysterical atmosphere of a revivalist meeting. This is all very well if you are trying to save a man's soul or convert a drunkard, but in this sense civilizations cannot be 'saved', they cannot take the pledge and from that moment never touch another drop. If one looks round the world today, the overheated imagination can find a dozen reasons for dismay, but if anything is certain it is that the collapse of our civilization will not come from any of the things which get into the headlines – not even from soil erosion. There will always be writers who like to frighten the human race; they used to write books for schoolboys, and were better employed doing so. Moreover, the identification of God's purpose (to speak in the Christian idiom) with the survival of our particular way of life is scarcely permissible. Of course we shall defend it with all our strength: that belongs to the way of life; but a world-picture which is merely projection of victory is of little value at a time of crisis or at any other time. In short, desperate urgency is something that belongs to a scale of events much smaller and less important than the scale Sir Walter has in mind: at bottom I find this a peculiarly faithless book. And further, a more profound diagnosis of our situation (such, for example, as appears in F. G. Juenger's book, *Die Perfektion der Technik*) would offer no place for the optimism that supposes that a 'revolution' can be conducted which would 'save' us. When what a man can get from the use and control of the natural world and his fellow men is the sole criterion of what he thinks he needs, there is no hope that the major part of mankind will find anything but good in this exploitation until it has been carried far enough to reveal its bitterness to the full. This, as we shall see in a moment, is not an argument for doing nothing, but it is a ground for not allowing ourselves to be comforted by the prospect, or even the possibility, of a revolution. The voyager in these waters is ill advised to weigh himself down with such heavy baggage; what he needs are things that will float with him when he is shipwrecked. Our situation, as I read it, is far more desperate than Sir Walter thinks, and at the same time it is far less to be alarmed about. And as for the bomb, no doubt we must consider it, but we should not allow it to unnerve us or we shall work ourselves into the state of mind which wishes that 'they would drop the damned thing and get it over'. In any case, the havoc wrought in Eastern Europe in the last few years is as bad as any atomic devastation; a powerful mass of deluded human beings is far more destructive than any bomb.

At bottom, of course, the crisis with which this book is concerned is not external, but emotional and intellectual. And even those who do not read the Sunday papers are aware of something that might be called critical in our situation. But it should be remembered that we have acquired excessively high standards, not only of physical and economic, but also of emotional and intellectual security, and judging our state of mind by these standards, we are apt to imagine in ourselves an altogether abnormal lack of coherence. If we are a generation which 'lives in an habitual consciousness of a world about to fall in on it', that is partly because we have unduly raised our standard of security. We look back at earlier periods in the history of our civilization and ascribe to them a world-picture far more coherent than they actually possessed, and by grossly exaggerating the emotional and intellectual stability of, for example, the Middle Ages or the nineteenth century, we attribute to ourselves a fictitious degree of insecurity. Other ages, no doubt, possessed more reliable habits of behaviour, but 'a clear image of the ends of human existence' has never been enjoyed except by a few rare individuals. And the notion that we are all at sea because as a society we have not got it, and that we should lay aside everything else in order to acquire it, is a piece of rationalistic exaggeration.

3

It is a sound rule in considering an argument to look closely at the minor premiss; that is the point at which most arguments go astray. The minor premiss of the argument of this book concerns the relationship between the university and the world, and it is not as clearly stated as one could wish. The university, it appears, should *reflect* the world; and from this point of view the 'crisis in the university' is its failure to do so. When we ask, What is this world which is to serve as a model? the answer we get is that it is a 'large-scale, mechanical civilization', that it is a 'democratic' world, that it is a world in which 'the sheer pace of events' has made 'planning' a necessity, that it is 'a world of insecurity', that intellectually and spiritually it is a world which has lost its confidence and sense of direction, and that it is 'explosive'. It is not denied that the universities have to some small extent succeeded in adapting themselves to this sort of world. In order to conform to the model, the whole balance of university studies has already suffered so great a change that what is new and 'in touch with the vital ideas of the age' has made the old pursuits of literature, philosophy and history 'seem secondary, remote and ineffectual'. Moreover, 'the essential part played by scientists in winning the war', combined with the incipient 'democratization of the universities', has 'produced in the public mind a more lively and sympathetic interest in the universities and a new sense of their value to the nation'. The process of adaptation has been slow, hesitating and inconsequent; but it has begun. To make the universities a reflection of the world means that 'the basic assumptions of the universities must be those of the nation', it means that they must have a 'more lively understanding of the major communal needs and of the significant communal changes actually occuring' – it means, in short, that the universities must accept and extrapolate the tendencies of the time.

Taken by itself, this ideal of a university which reflects fully and accurately the world as it has come to be is, of course, nothing better than an unconditional surrender to the absence of discrimination which, elsewhere, is taken to be characteristic of the world today. A world moved by the plausible ethics of productivity is willing to endow the universities in order that they may co-operate in the good work of carrying the 'crisis' a step further. And the business of the universities is to conform to the conditions of the endowment. The world is 'explosive', therefore the universities should explode. This clearly is a trifle too naïve a view of the relationship of university and world, and consequently a second duty is promulgated: the duty of providing 'leadership'. This duty is interpreted as something more than merely that of being the first to explode. It is the duty of providing a new world-picture, an ideology to give us back our confidence, a gospel to save the world from itself. To perform this second duty the university must be relieved from the immediate pressure of the world; its inspiration must be something other than the way the world is at present going.

This dual relationship of the university and the world raises the obvious question which, so far as I can find, Sir Walter never considers: the question, what happens to this judicious scheme if the relation of reflection and the relation of guidance conflict with one another? My own view of the matter is that the conflict today is absolute; but without insisting upon that, there is a remarkable absence from this book of any attempt to establish an even plausible harmony between the two. And this incoherence affects the argument at many points. Two examples may be given. Consider the relationship between 'the student' and the university as it appears here, leaving on one side for the moment the extraordinary portrait of 'the student' which emerges. It is suggested that today the undergraduate looks up and is not fed. A variety of reasons is given for this failure, but in interpreting it this book never decides whether it is because the undergraduate's alleged search for certainty, for a philosophy of life which the world does not provide, is left unprovided also in the university, or because the undergraduate comes with a mind already filled with the prevailing philosophy of indiscrimination and finds the university out of touch with his already formed conclusions. Either of these is a plausible reason for discontent; you may lack guidance and find in the university a hesitating and indecisive guide, or you may find in it an imperfect reflection of what you have already taken to be your guide or of your own mental instability, but the two states of mind are exclusive of one another. You may say, 'out there in the street something new is in the making, which will shatter all the syllogisms and formulae of the schools; conform or get out of the way', or you may say, 'out there in the street is chaos, please help me to distinguish the good from the bad' – but you cannot reasonably say both at once. 'In order to be useful to the community,' says Sir Walter, 'the university must retain a large measure of autonomy against the community', and he hopes that by calling this a 'paradox' he can have the best of both worlds. But it is not paradoxical at all: on the one view of the relationship of university and world it is clearly false, on the other it is truism.

The same incoherence runs through the treatment which the doctrine of 'scientific humanism' receives in this book. This doctrine (which, it may be observed, is a doctrine *about* science and technology and is not itself in any sense 'scientific') is obviously attractive to Sir Walter because it appears of combine both views

of the relationship of university and world. In the first place, it is a
doctrine which directly reflects 'what is most vital in contemporary
culture', and its defenders wish to carry out to the full the desired
adaptation of the university to the world. And secondly, it is a
doctrine which appears to offer an alternative to the prevailing
intellectual chaos; it provides 'integration'. And on account of both
these characteristics it is found to have 'high merits'. The 'scientific
humanists' are said to have been 'more responsibly awake than the
rest of us to the significance of changes in the modern world, to
revolutionary possibilities of human control of events, and the
relation of what goes on in the university to what goes on outside
it'. They are praised for their 'social conscience'. And yet 'scientific
humanism' is placed among the 'spurious remedies'. It turns out
to be a naïve assertion of the plausible ethics of indiscriminate
productivity, a simplehearted worship of power, an innocent bow-
ing down before the mighty course of events. It turns out to have
no criterion for helping us to know when we are not hungry. But
why was this not recognized at first? Why all this elaborate falling
over backwards in order to find merit in what is worthless? Because,
I think, Sir Walter has confused himself by trying to hold on to
two conflicting purposes, and because he is unable to distinguish
between doctrine and rhetoric. The *doctrine* of 'scientific humanism'
in respect of the universities is the acceptance, without misgiving
or qualification, of the view that 'the basic assumptions of the
university must be those of the nation', the view that a world
wedded to the enterprise of limitless technological improvement
should have co-operative universities. And this conforms exactly to
Sir Walter's first demand. The *rhetoric*, on the other hand, is that of
discrimination, though the values are studiously ambiguous –
bigger, faster, more democratic, international, a freer kind of
freedom, the universities in alliance with 'all the forces making for
social progress'. And this seems to satisfy Sir Walter's second
demand. But in fact, it is only a rhetorical satisfaction: this is not a
moral doctrine, to be considered in relation to other moral doctrines; it is the assertion, disguised in the rhetoric of a moral ideal,
that moral judgement is unnecessary. The 'scientific humanist' is
not awake to the significance of changes in the modern world; he is
merely awake to the changes. This is not a new situation; it is as
old as the race. What man needs from the natural world is what he
thinks he can get from it. In itself there is nothing moral in this
process of exploitation; if it is to be moral it has to be moralized,
and morality is being in command of the situation, is being able to
discriminate, is knowing when you are not hungry.

In the long run, no doubt, universities will always come to be some sort of a reflection of the world in which they exist. They cannot be insulated from that world, and the world is likely to have the final voice. A war, a Royal Commission, a Barlow Committee, a specific benefaction, a government grant, each involves the approximation of a university to something in the world outside; pressure is continuous and no pressure is neutral, no gift is without strings, and the politician loves the unseen string. But merely to be in the fashion and to accept what comes is no very exalted ideal, and a university which has power to refuse a benefaction thought to be eccentric to its character must, when it exercises that power, have some sense of its own character and identity. This character may change, it certainly has changed, but what is to be avoided is change of such a kind that the university loses its sense of identity. The doctrine that the university should move step for step with the world, at the same speed and partaking in every eccentricity of the world's fashion, refusing nothing that is offered, responsive to every suggestion, is a piece of progressive superstition and not to be tolerated by any sane man. Keeping up to date with the world is, then, an ideal which is subject to two important qualifications: the world must offer something which at least seems to be desirable as a model to be copied by an existing university, and the activity of approximation must be carried out in a manner that does not entail a loss of identity. Opinions may differ about our present situation. My own view is that the contemporary world offers no desirable model for a university, and that the current activity of approximation is lacking, not in speed, but in discrimination. Sir Walter's opinion appears to be that not to move with the times is itself a significant failure. He deplores the fact that those who are 'in tune with the movement of ideas in the contemporary world' are so small a number in the universities; the 'new scientific culture' would have already gone much further if it had been properly welcomed. And he thinks that now is the time to stage a revolution which shall at the same time rapidly bring the universities up to date and fit them to provide what the world lacks.

4

There can be little doubt that much of the incoherence of this book springs from the fact that the argument is a communal product; too many different views have had to be incorporated and each with some sort of approval. And while we may pass over minor inconsistencies (and a certain amount of ordinary silliness), there are more important blemishes which call for notice. Every page of the book testifies to an unqualified belief in the value of criticism and self-criticism. The project of uncovering everything, of thinking out afresh the whole aim and basis of the university with a view to making a new start, is regarded not merely as desirable but as a necessity if we are to have a lively and responsive institution. Not to embark upon this project is to be guilty of 'sloppy thinking' and 'conventional prejudice'. There will be many who have no difficulty in consenting to this opinion, and, for the sake of argument, I am prepared to accept it. But it must be observed that there are occasions in this book when the desirability of being awake and responsive to what is going on are interpreted in so extreme a manner that one is reminded of Godwin's wish to make his blood flow voluntarily. Nobody would be so foolish as to deny the value of a critical attitude towards things, but surely it is a little wanton to say that 'ceaseless criticism, from without as well as from within, is necessary for the university's health': *ceaseless* criticism never did anyone or anything any good; it unnerves the individual and distracts the institution.

But the thesis of the book does not stop there; not only is criticism necessary and revolution essential, but we are told that *now* is the moment for the inquest and the reform. Undergraduate education has never been thought out as a whole, it has been shaped by the pressure of circumstances and not by clear thought directed to definite ends; but now is the time to embark upon this piece of thinking and to set on foot the changes necessary to implement its results. And, not unreasonably, we look for some convincing arguments in support of this remarkable view. There are, I think, two possible arguments, either of which would be pretty convincing; if it were shown that the universities at the present time were hopelessly corrupt, a danger to themselves and to the whole society, or if it were shown that the present time offered remarkably good prospects for fruitful reform, the case for radical reform now could be considered to have been established. The book, on the whole, relies on the second of these arguments. It is true that we are told that the time at our disposal is short – which takes us back to the atomic bomb or to soil erosion. But the general point of view seems to be: because the world is upside down, it is the most profitable moment to turn the universities inside out.

The precise arguments which appear are instructive: there are two of them. It is suggested, first, that this is the moment for the enterprise of university reform because it would be carried on the great wave of 'social planning' which at the moment is sweeping us forward to a new and better world. We have at the moment a clearer idea of what we mean by 'social needs' and 'social justice' than ever before, and consequently the time is ripe to apply it to the universities. This, if I may say so, is nonsense; the current interpretation of 'social needs' is narrower, more eccentric and less coherent than it has been for centuries. And if it were true, what becomes of all this talk of a civilization which has lost its sense of direction? Sir Walter takes what we call 'planning' as evidence of vitality and confidence, but it may with more justice be taken as a symptom of our absence of direction and our loss of dependable habits of behaviour. But the second argument is more important because it is one of the most mischievous fallacies passing for sense at the present time. We have just emerged from a state of total war, therefore (the argument runs) it is the most favourable moment for carrying out profitable reforms in every part of society. Years ago, Karl Mannheim told us that 'by making the necessary adaptations to the needs of war one does not always realize that very often they contain also the principles of adaptation to the needs of the New Age', and ever since every reformer in a hurry has disingenuously taken up the cry: every crisis is hailed as a God-given opportunity to remodel society. And we are told here that the task of adjusting the universities to the world, the project of taking the universities to pieces and putting them together again, may most profitably be undertaken now because we have just emerged from a war. And further, we are told that our experience of war is the most reliable guide to the activity of university reform: 'the analogy of wartime experience suggests that, to get the most out of a university, it must be enrolled in the service of some cause beyond itself'. These are the disintegrating politics of the 'Dunkirk spirit'.

Now, we cannot too often remind ourselves that, in politics and in every other activity, war offers the least fruitful opportunity for profitable change: war is a blind guide to civilized life. In war all that is most superficial in our tradition is encouraged merely because it is useful, even necessary, for victory. *Inter arma silent leges* is an old adage which can support a wide interpretation; not only are the laws suspended, but the whole balance of the society is disturbed. There are many who have no other idea of social progress than the extrapolation of the character of a society in time of war – the artificial unity, the narrow overmastering purpose, the devotion to a single cause and the subordination of everything to it – all this seems to them inspiring: but the direction of their admiration reveals the emptiness of their souls. Not only is a society which has just emerged from a shattering war in the worst possible position for making profitable reforms in the universities, but the inspiration of war itself is the most misleading of all inspirations in such an enterprise. If there is anything left standing with even a moderate degree of stability (and Sir Walter admits, rather grudgingly, that there is greater stability in British universities at the present time than in any others), let it remain for the moment; it is something to lean upon. To set about adjusting the universities to a world in chaos will make certain that they will be approximated to all that is most trivial in our tradition. Every proposal for change which springs directly from an emergency is unavoidably governed by what is temporary and accidental.[2] Nor is this mere theory: the major 'adjustment' which the universities have already suffered, which has resulted in the desperate overcrowding at the present time, has done them more damage than any 'failure to meet the needs of the time'. Oddly enough, Sir Walter pays very little attention to the 'crisis in the university' which springs from the altogether excessive number of undergraduates,[3] and he assumes that every unprejudiced man will agree with the findings of the Barlow Committee. There is, then, no harm in thinking about the true aims and basis of a university, though the present prospects of reaching profitable conclusions are dim; but beyond question this is the worst of all moments for promoting radical changes to bring the universities into line with what is going on in the world. In the end, the only plausible argument in favour of choosing the present time for such an enterprise is the current political argument that, in a world so chaotic a small addition to the disorder will scarcely be noticed, and if things go wrong circumstances are waiting to take the blame.

5

We have observed already the general terms of Sir Walter Moberly's reading of the 'crisis in the university': it springs from the slowness with which the universities of this country are adjusting themselves to the changes which have taken place in the world outside, and from their failure to provide the necessary guidance. It is time now to consider this diagnosis more closely. The condition of the universities is said to be one of chaos. They do not know what they are 'for', and they have never thought about

[2] This is the main reason for the eccentricities of the Forestry Commission.
[3] *The Problem of the Universities*: Nuffield College Report.

the matter. They offer a moderately efficient education in various specialisms, but since there is no point in the university at which a synoptic view of the intellectual world is attempted, or even suggested, the prevailing appearance is that of a miscellaneous collection of fragments. Nobody is incited to want (much less, to acquire) 'a unified conception of life'; nobody is given any assistance to 'decide responsibly on a life purpose'. The universities, being without any self-conscious, single view of the world, offer no 'overmastering experience'.

The cause of all this is not far to seek: it lies in the intellectual and moral disabilities of the dons. Except for the 'scientific humanists' – who are approved, not for what they say, but merely because they speak – there is a conspiracy of silence on all the important questions of the day. The dons are mere specialists; they have no 'philosophy', and they are reluctant to engage in the sort of self-examination which might lead them to acquire a 'philosophy'. Self-defeated simpletons, they do not recognize that to say nothing about things in general is 'a mark of personal incapacity'. And worse, they excuse their lack of interest in anything but their own specialisms by affecting a sham neutrality when asked about anything of 'real importance'. They are lazy, pusillanimous, evasive, irresponsible shirkers when it comes to thinking about 'the burning questions of the day'. Those who are not 'elegant triflers' are too dull to play even that unexacting part. Indolent, proud and resentful, their lectures written and unwilling to change them, their minds fixed in the rut of their specialism, they are as 'remote and ineffectual' as the world has always supposed them to be.

Now, what is to be thought of this indictment – when the necessary allowances have been made for exaggeration? I think Sir Walter's shots may be considered to compose a moderately compact group, but unfortunately they are on the edge of the target. As we shall see later, he scores one 'bull', but since it falls so far outside the group it detracts from the total effect. In other words, this indictment springs almost inevitably from Sir Walter's assumptions, but its strength is limited to their cogency. What these assumptions are appears in the remedy proposed.

The inspiration of the remedy is the belief that any university which is without a single self-conscious purpose, inexorably pursued, must be failing in the task of being a university. It is impossible for a university to plan its studies or its corporate life except by reference to some standard of values, and 'it is impossible to have a rational standard of values in the absence of any clear image of the ends of human existence, and that entails some conception of the nature of man and of the world'. And a university whose 'working philosophy' is surreptitious 'will be wanting in intellectual honesty'. This inspiration, of course, makes certain that nothing will be recognized as valuable which is not self-consciously present; what is not expressly designed to be there may be assumed to be absent. And consequently, in my opinion, we start on the wrong foot, with the assumption that we were born yesterday and that the universities are without the advantage of traditions or a sense of their own character. But further, it brings us up against that most difficult problem of 'planning' – the difficulty that nothing can be decided until everything has been decided. If you cannot determine the 'correct number of nurses' until you have determined the correct number to be employed in every other occupation, how are you to make a start? Aristotle solved the problem centuries ago by pointing out that no sane man ever goes about anything in this manner; he does not assume a blank sheet, and he is not such a fool as to suppose that he cannot enjoy his porridge, or even educate his son, until he has solved the riddle of the universe. But Aristotle is now among the less frequently read writers; for two centuries we have gone to school instead with the Germans – the only European people which did start more or less with a blank sheet and became philosophers before they had learned how to live – and we have come to believe in the preposterous doctrine that you must first catch your *Weltanschauung*. However, it seems clear enough that 'when we turn to the primary questions, concering the things that really make or mar a university, and ask, What are universities for? What effect should they have on their alumni? What are their responsibilities to the outside world? we are asking questions to which a minority of university teachers return discordant answers and the majority return no clear answers at all.' And consequently the remedy must be a revolutionary change.

Now, mixed in with this doctrine of the necessity of revolutionary adjustment under the guidance of a self-conscious purpose, there is in this book another doctrine to the effect that 'the clue to reconstruction is to be found in our tradition'. How these two can be made to agree, I cannot say; but the treatment which the traditions of British university education receive here accounts for the small reliance Sir Walter places upon them. A chapter is given to an examination of what is called 'the changing conceptions of the university's task'. But a recognizable university never appears on the scene, because the hiatus between the formulated conception of a university – as expounded by Newman or Whewell or Paulsen or Matthew Arnold – and the sort of education a university actually provided at different times, is never observed. These 'conceptions of the university's task' are all very well in their way, but it is forgotten that they originate nothing except an illusory sense of understanding what it is all about, and the actual university escapes between the lines. Theories of this sort may be contrasted neatly with one another, they may be said to 'displace' or to 'supersede' one another; but a history of theories is not a history of university education: neither Newman's nor Matthew Arnold's university (any more than feudalism or a *laissez-faire* economy) ever existed. And to contrast a university as it exists today with a theory of what it was yesterday or the day before, is to institute a comparison between things which do not match one another. The real reason why a movement 'back' to any to these 'conceptions of the university's task' is impossible, is not because they are out of date, but because they never existed. We have today, says Sir Walter, 'a chaotic university', but, by focusing his attention on theories, he has concealed from himself the fact that there never was anything else but a chaotic university. This, I think, is the reason for his misinterpretation of what he calls the tradition of 'Classical Humanism': for him it is a 'conception of the university's task' in which 'the function of the university was to train a ruling class' and to provide for 'those professions which have, or used to have, most social prestige'. Because he sees it only as a theory (it is even so emasculated that it is made to exist independently of the Christian element in European civilization), the tradition of 'Classical Humanism' is said to be 'bound up with a society based upon privilege'; he even pictures Oxford and Cambridge as engaged until yesterday in educating a 'leisured class', and finds that this great education in Christian-Classical culture somehow conflicts with 'the unsatisfied demands of social justice'. With the bogus boldness of those who say, 'These things have come to stay; we must accept them', this book too often surrenders to all that is worst in the current disingenuous cant. It suggests that by putting 'social' in front of 'justice' something significant has been said, it accepts the current identification of unselfishness with equalitarianism and it extends an undiscriminating approval to all those who claim to be allied with 'all the forces making for social progress'. And what is this leisured class? It appears to be the class of Peel and Gladstone, both of whom, it is well known, led lives of ease and indolence. The notion that it is something new that the vast majority of undergraduates leaving the universities have to earn a living is pure fantasy, and the suggestion that those who do not earn their living unavoidably engage in worthless activity is preposterous. Indeed, the pages in which the university education of twenty, fifty or a hundred years ago are discussed are obscured quite unaccountably by a sense almost of guilt.

Given the diagnosis of the chaos and the inspiration of the remedy, the character of the remedy is obvious. A university, if it is to fulfil the tast assigned to it, must abandon its shy neutrality, overcome its inhibitions and acquire 'a recognizable and conscious orientation'. The discussion of 'ultimate questions' of 'real intellectual issues', of the burning questions of the days', from being considered improper, must be recognized as a fundamental responsibility. Nothing should be taboo. And further, 'there must be some point in the university' where the necessity of acquiring a 'philosophy of life' is urged upon the undergraduate and where he is given the necessary help to acquire one. At the present time he is directionless and leaderless; the university should see to it that he is given an idea that 'grips' him. He desires to be saved by momentous experience; the university must provide the experience, an experience such as J. S. Mill describes as coming to him from reading Bentham: 'I now had opinions and a creed, a doctrine, a philosophy...'. Instead of remaining merely a polytechnic (which is what it has degenerated into), the university must provide a synoptic, integrated view of the moral and intellectual world, it must 'teach a unified conception of life'.

Now, all this looks like a plea for what we are accustomed to call an ideology, and the appearance seems to be confirmed when we read that the 'recognizable and conscious orientation of the university' should 'take the form of a common moral outlook or *Weltanschauung* which sees the challenge of our time in personalist rather than technical terms, which, though not specifically Christian, is 'christianized' in that it has been deeply influenced by Christianity, and which is a basis on which Christians and large numbers of non-Christians can work cordially together'. Elsewhere, however, the project of a university designed to put over an ideology is disclaimed – 'it is no part of the duty of a university to inculcate any particular philosophy of life. But it is its duty to assist its students to form their own philosophies of life, so that they may not go out into the world maimed and useless.' But for two reasons this disclaimer is unconvincing: first, the whole view put before us – briefly, that every man without a philosophy of life is 'maimed and useless' – is itself an ideology and one of the narrowest and most absurd; and secondly, it is clear that Sir Walter thinks we should be better off if we had an agreed ideology which embraced everything, if we had a precise answer to every question and a neat place for every experience. A coherent system 'reminiscent of St Thomas's *Summa*' is, alas, at the moment impossible, but it is represented as a legitimate 'long-term objective'. How revealing is this nostalgic backward glance to an imaginary world from which chaos had been excluded. And how stupendous is this misunderstanding of the *Summa Theologica*, turning it into what a recent writer has called 'a sort of staff-college doctrine', which it never was except in the minds of the ideologues. The magnitude and importance of the 'issues' and 'questions' to be discussed in the university is frequently impressed upon us in this book, but we are left in some doubt about their precise character. Indeed, like the novelist who, writing of 'orgies of unimaginable vice', convinces us that he has an innocent imagination, Sir Walter never leaves the high road of generality. The 'master question', round which the university should revolve, appears to be 'How shall a man live?', and I suppose it is not an exaggeration to speak of this as 'fundamental'. How profitably it can be discussed, and what sort of an answer may be expected, is another matter. But in default of more exact specification, one is left with the impression that under the new regime the universities would degenerate into that most worthless of all conditions – that of a forum for the discussion of ideologies. And as for these 'burning questions', I suspect they are the sort which give a faint flicker round about midnight and have burnt themselves out by the next morning. By all means let them be discussed, but let us also be aware of their triviality: no question is inherently 'burning', and the most probable way of making an important question trivial is by hotting it up.

A variety of means by which this remedy may be applied is offered in this book. Obviously what will be needed is a more responsible and a more articulate sort of don, and the case for tests and terms of subscription is examined with some care. In the end they are rejected, with the proviso that if one is a member of an appointments committee one should not give one's vote to a candidate whom one suspects of bad faith or intellectual dishonesty. An enhanced community life for students, such as may spring from properly organized halls of residence, and extended means of communication between staff and students in different faculties, are expected to promote the purpose ascribed to the university. But the main emphasis is on the reform of the curriculum of studies and the methods of teaching. There should be widened professional courses (so that the doctor should be taught something about 'life' as well as about medicine), Honours Schools combining more than one subject should be developed, the possibilities of 'broad-based general Degree Courses', such as exist in American universities, should be explored. But, above all, in the effort to integrate the fragmentary specialisms of the contemporary university, there should be single integrating courses of lectures, which 'pose to the students the problems of a philosophy of life, and, it may be, offer a solution'. Sir Walter is, in general, sceptical of the value of lectures, but allows them merit if they possess a 'dynamic quality'.

Now, within the assumptions of this book, these are all sensible suggestions. The main assumptions are: that there is only one good sort of university education – a didactic training in the current ideologies with a view to selecting the best; that there is only one good sort of university – that which has a single, clearly defined, self-conscious purpose; that there is only one good sort of communal organization – that in which students live in halls of residence or colleges; that there is only one good sort of don – the man or woman who is intensely interested in 'the burning questions of the day' and is capable of being articulate about them, a Hippias Polyhistor;[4] that there is only one good sort of student – the man or woman who is interested in 'problems' and who wants a 'philosophy of life'; that there is only one good sort of lecture – the 'dynamic' sort; and that it may be safely assumed that unless a purpose is consciously pursued it will never be achieved. It is a remarkable performance for so liberal a mind; one may only conclude that he has dwelt so long on one thought that it has taken him prisoner. Consider the view that unless you expressly aim at something it will never be achieved. Nothing could be more manifestly false a generalization. Those who look with suspicion on an achievement because it was not part of the design will, in the end, find themselves having to be suspicious of all the greatest human achievements. The doctrine that a thing either does not exist or at least is worthless if it is not planned, and that unforeseen consequences of activity are a sign of failure, is a piece of extravagance. Consider the don and the student. It appears from these pages that not to be interested in a *Weltanschuauung*, indeed not to be interested in politics, is a sure sign of incapacity in the one and dullness in both – and at one stroke the best and the worst of the human race are written off as a dead loss. As it happens I am interested in these things, but I know that there are others, much better educated than myself and more reliable members of society, who never give them a thought. To impute irresponsibility and

4 Plato, *Hippias Minor*, 368.

evasiveness to these people is arrogant folly. The current, almost universal, speculative interest in morals and politics is not a sign of health and is not a cure for the disease we suffer from; it is only a symptom of disorder. And it seems never to have occurred to the author of this book that one of the effects of all the planning of the universities of the last twenty-five years has been to make certain that a man such as Lowes-Dickinson can never again exist in Cambridge; the destruction that has gone on in the name of integration is lamentable. Consider these 'dynamic' lecturers. A university would be poor if it had no preacher, and a preacher who is inspiring is worth more than one who is only instructive. But he will never be the most valuable member of the university. And if there is a quack about the place, if there is an intellectual crook, you may be certain that he will not lack dynamism; I should have thought we had had enough of that dangerous quality for the time being. Anyone who knows anything about a university knows that even the meanest has room for a dozen different sorts of lecturer. And when I look back upon the great teachers I have heard – to Burkitt, Lapsley, Coulton, Cornford, McTaggart – none of them was dynamic and only one cared a straw about a *Weltanschauung*. I would rather listen to Bury 'drone from a dull manuscript in a voice inaudible beyond the front two benches', than to a self-conscious quack retailing some vulgar and trivial message. Consider, lastly, the notion that the best sort of university is one in which the students are housed in colleges or halls of residence. Anyone who has spent his undergraduate days in Oxford or in Cambridge knows the great value of a residential university; it is something that belongs to our tradition and we know how to manage it. But anyone who has experienced, for example, life in the university quarter of a German town, knows the value, even the blessed relief, in *not* belonging to a tightly organized community, and that it is an unpardonable prejudice to suppose that, in this respect, there is only one good sort of university. Let us have none of this fanaticism.

6

No one can hope to say anything significant about the universities unless he understands that university education is neither a beginning nor an end, but a middle. Hobbes's pronouncement that 'the instruction of the people, depends wholly, on the teaching of Youth in the Universities' is not true, and he ought to have known better than to have made it. No man begins his education at the university, he begins it in the nursery; and a man's formative years are not at an end when he takes his degree. The character of a university is, therefore, in part determined by the sort of undergraduate who appears – not, of course, by the idiosyncracies of individuals but by the assumptions that may safely be made about the general run, about their age, their intellectual standards, their moral upbringing and their ambitions. The main difference between British and American universities springs from the difference between British and American homes and schools. Of course, universities have some control over the sort of undergraduate who appears, but it is a limited and a remote control. Hitherto (until yesterday), in spite of great changes, the universities of Britain had something valuable to offer which the undergraduates who appeared in them could make use of because it was rooted in, generally speaking, accurate assumptions about the sort of undergraduate who would appear. What they had to offer was not something which only one social class could appreciate, or something suitable only to a 'leisured class'; undergraduates who came with a variety of tastes, bents, predispositions and ambitions could find in what was offered something recognizably appropriate to themselves.

The university offered, in the first place, a limited variety of studies. Where this particular selection came from, it would be hard to say. Probably no one of these subjects of study was capable of defence on *a priori* grounds; no university ever drew up the curriculum with a known and adequate reason for every entry. Some of these studies were of distant origin and owed their place in the universities to quite different reasons from those which could now be used to defend them. (For example, the place and importance of Classics in the school and university education of the sixteenth century was mainly on account of the positive knowledge contained in the writings of Greek and Latin authors; they were *modern* studies.) Others were comparatively new and could still be defended on the grounds which had won them their place. Certainly none of these studies was designed for any purpose so definite as to fit a 'ruling class' to rule or a mercantile class to conduct business. Indeed, the only character common to them all was that of being a recognized branch of scholarship. And this was true also of the three studies which had a professional appearance – theology, law and medicine. For in the universities these were not a merely professional training; they were a preludial education to which apprenticeship elsewhere had to be added. They did not survive because of the 'social prestige' of the professions with which they were connected, but because each of them, like every other study in the universities, was a recognized branch of learning. And the new subjects, which had been added from time to time, claimed entry on the ground that each involved standards of scholarship comparable to those of the subjects already admitted. An undergraduate, then, if he wished it, could find in the studies offered at the universities something at least not remote from his chosen profession; and if he had made no definite choice, he could find something to interest him, or, if he had the tastes of a scholar, something to captivate him. Each of those studies was a specialism, but none was a very narrow specialism. There was, in general, no heated discussion about the relations between these special studies, chiefly because (except to those with speculative tastes) each was easily recognized as belonging to the single world of learning. Looking back on it, the impression I seem to have received (though I did not then embody it in this image) was that of a conversation in which each study had a distinctive voice – a conversation which occasionally degenerated into an argument (for example, between 'science' and 'religion'), but which in the main retained its proper character. Nobody then gave lessons in the art of conversation itself; that was to be learnt by listening to the conversation (an activity for which it was assumed the undergraduate had already been prepared), and only a Sophist would have considered the art of conversation to be a separate *techne*. The university was neither an institute in which only one voice was to be heard, nor was it a polytechnic in which only the mannerisms of the voices were taught. There was, then, an atmosphere of study; each undergraduate was pursuing, within the range of his own capabilities, some recognized branch of learning. The small number of undergraduates who came to the universities for reasons altogether extraneous to study may be disregarded. Some provision was made for them; they were not by any means valueless members of the society, but they did not profoundly influence the curriculum of the university.

Secondly, the British university offered a field of extra-academic activity within the traditions of British life; clubs and societies to which succeeding generations belonged, the opportunity of forming new associations, the room and the means of pursuing a great variety of interests, social, athletic, artistic, religious and scholarly. Here too the undergraduate could follow his taste or ambition according to his means and exercise his energies; here also was an inheritance to be enjoyed. And of this no more need be said.

But thirdly, the university had something to offer equally to every undergraduate, and I take this to be its most characteristic gift because it was something exclusive to the university and rooted in the character of university education as a middle. A man may at any time in his life begin to explore a new branch of learning or engage in fresh activity, but only at a university can he do this without a rearrangement of his scarce resources of time and energy: in later life he is already committed to so much that he cannot easily throw off. The great and characteristic gift of the university was the gift of an interval. Here was an opportunity to put aside the hot allegiances of youth without the necessity of acquiring new loyalties to take their place. Here was an interval in which a man might refuse to commit himself. Here was a break in the tyrannical course of irreparable events; a period in which to look round upon the world without the sense of an enemy at one's back or the insistent pressure to make up one's mind; a moment in which one was relieved of the necessity of 'coming to terms with oneself' or of entering the fiercely trivial partisan struggles of the world outside; a moment in which to taste the mystery without the necessity of at once seeking a solution.[5] Here, indeed, was the opportunity to exercise, and perhaps to cultivate, the highest and most easily destroyed of human capacities, what Keats called 'negative capability' – 'when a man is capable of being in uncertainties, mysteries, doubts, without any irritable racing after fact and reason' – an opportunity to practise that 'suspended judgement' of which the 'neutrality' of liberalism is so pale a shadow. And all this, not in an intellectual vacuum, but surrounded by all the inherited learning and literature and experience of our civilization; not as a sole occupation, but combined with the discipline of studying some recognized branch of learning; and neither as a first step in education, for those wholly ignorant of how to behave or think, nor as a final education to fit a man for the day of judgement, but as a middle.

It would be difficult to determine the generation of this remarkable opportunity; certainly nobody planned it or even considered it in the abstract. It was a by-product. Perhaps it sprang (as Lucretius imagines human limbs to have sprung) from there being people who, in varying degrees, could make use of it. At all events, I think it was the one thing which every university in Europe, in some measure, provided, and in virtue of which, more than of anything else, it was a university. The enjoyment of it depended, of course, upon some previous preparation (no man ignorant of what he should have been taught in the nursery could expect to enjoy it),

[5] Plato, *Laws*, 888.

but it did not depend upon any definable pre-existing privilege or upon the absence of the necessity of earning one's living in the end – it was itself the privilege of being a 'student', the enjoyment of *schole*. One might, if one were so inclined, reduce this to a doctrine about the character of a university; one might call it the doctrine of the interim. But the doctrine would be no more than a brief expression of what it felt like to be an undergraduate on that first October morning. Almost overnight, a world of ungracious fact has melted into infinite possiblility; we, who belonged to no 'leisured class', had been freed for a moment from the curse of Adam, the burdensome distinction between work and play. What opened before us was not a road but a boundless sea; and it was enough to stretch one's sails to the wind. The distracting urgency of an immediate destination was absent, duty no longer oppressed, boredom and disappointment were words without meaning, death was unthinkable. And it seemed as if desire had resolved itself into the original, undifferentiated appetite from which it sprang, and that limitless energy was again let loose. Of course, this appetite would have to surrender its formlessness and this energy find a direction; but there was time enough for that: the interim was ours. For the moment we were able to step aside from the brittle formulations of the world, from the current vulgar estimates of its predicament, from the 'burning questions' and the world's slick answers. But it belongs to the character of an interim to come to an end; there is a time for everything and nothing should be prolonged beyond its time. The eternal undergraduate is a lost soul. It was possible that, in the end, we were better able to deal with the world, it was possible that the knowledge we acquired could be coverted into power, but these were not the motives of the experience nor the criteria by which its value should be judged. Indeed, I think the experience could never come to anyone who had already subscribed to that most dismal of all sentiments: *scientia propter potentiam*. Contentment, says Fuller, 'is the one property which is required of those who seek the philosopher's stone; they must not do it with any covetous desire, for otherwise they shall never find it.' This university did not turn out men who had completely come to terms with themselves, men who had 'settled' all their problems. It recognized and had a place for minds that were not and never would be *problematisch*. A man in his undergraduate days might be expected to discover the triviality of some 'problems', he might hope to have enjoyed, some time or another, a glimpse of a vista which, we suppose, terminates in 'a clear image of the ends of human existence', but if he had a settled 'philosophy of life' in his pocket on the day he took his degree, it was to be supposed that he had come by it improperly.

Now, there are various ways in which a crisis may overtake a university of this sort. First, if there was no longer anybody who could appreciate and make use of what if offered, such a university would find itself without undergraduates. This, I think, is an improbable state of affairs in England in the near future. Anyone who has worked in a contemporary overcrowded university knows it to be an illusion that there was any large untapped reserve of men and women who could make use of this kind of university but who never had the opportunity of doing so. But, so far as my observation goes, it appears that there are about as many as there ever were (but no more) to whom the gifts of a university seem valuable. How long this will continue to be so is doubtful; the way things are going is not friendly to the existence of this sort of undergraduate.

Secondly, if such a university were flooded with undergraduates who were unprepared and had no use for the opportunities offered, or if there were men abroad who had the power and the intention to destroy, by one means or another, such a university, it would not be unduly alarmist to proclaim a state of crisis. This needs to be considered carefully, because a crisis of this sort has ceased to be a mere possibility. Let us first investigate the character of the contemporary undergraduate. It cannot be said that Sir Walter Moberly gives us anything but an incoherent picture of him. Leaving aside the allegation that he is essentially *problematisch*, that he has a longing for 'certainty' about this world and the next and above all about himself, what are we told? We are told that he 'knows more' than his predecessor, that he is 'more highly selected', that 'on the average he is more able', that he is 'potentially better material'. There is, of course, a certain ambiguity here, but in general it may be said that this is emphatically not true. If he 'knows more' it is only in respect of some relatively narrow specialism, on the average the contemporary undergraduate is not 'more able' than his predecessor, and the tests by which he has been selected are not those which have much bearing upon his ability to make use of the sort of university we are considering. But further, not only is this picture, on the whole, false; it is contradicted by the rest of what Sir Walter has to say. For we are told that the modern undergraduate 'has not the background of culture which could once be assumed', that his 'range of interest is more circumscribed', that he has 'little initiative or resilience', that his aim is 'utilitarian', and that he looks upon the university 'first and foremost as the avenue to a desirable job'. He is said to be antipathetic to the sort of detachment which the universities have cultivated; and the 'abler and more altruistic' among them, 'the leading students' are eager to engage in the affairs of the world and to turn study into politics. Some of this Sir Walter falsely ascribes to 'pressing material preoccupation'; but whatever the reason for this alleged change of character, the result is manifestly an undergraduate who is less able to make use of the sort of university we are considering. Nor is this all. From the outside we have men of power who desire that the universities should be flooded with exactly this sort of undergraduate, whose character they admire; they have the intention of transforming the universities into places designed and planned to provide what these undergraduates suppose they need. Here, I think, are the makings of a genuine crisis in the universities. For when the pressure of change in this direction becomes irresistible, the universities will suffer a destructive metamorphosis from which recovery will be impossible. The problem today is *not* 'how to translate the ideal of the cultivated gentleman into democratic terms and combine an intensive and relentless pursuit of excellence with a new sensitiveness to the demands of social justice'. In the past a rising class was aware of something valuable enjoyed by others which it wished to share; but this is not so today. The leaders of the rising class are consumed with a contempt for everything which does not spring from their own desires, they are convinced in advance that they have nothing to learn and everything to teach, and consequently their aim is loot – to appropriate to themselves the organization, the shell of the institution, and convert it to their own purposes. The problem of the universities today is how to avoid destruction at the hands of men who have no use for their characteristic virtues, men who are convinced only that 'knowledge is power'.[6]

There is, however, a third direction from which a crisis, or something like it, may overtake a university: if the universities, in respect of matters still within their control, were ceasing to offer what they had hitherto given. Here Sir Walter has something relevant to say, and a little that is helpful. He sees a danger in what he calls 'the overloading of curricula'; and there can be no doubt that this would be destruction of the sort of university we are considering. It is not a matter entirely within the control of a university – almost the whole of the alien pressure from which the universities suffer is in this direction – but something could and should be done to ease the burden. But Sir Walter's diagnosis is

[6] Ernest Green, *Education for a New Society* (London: George Routledge and Sons, 1947).

imperfect, and he gives the wrong reason for thinking that the current excessive demands on the undergraduate are evil. First, what he objects to is merely the overloading of the *specialist* curricula; he wants to add what he calls 'integrative courses of lectures', which, though they appear to be 'compulsory', for some obscure reason he does not regard as increasing the academic burden. And secondly, an overloaded curriculum seems to him an evil, not because it prevents a university offering its most precious gift (though he does say that it reduces the time available for the undergraduate to 'stand and stare'), but mainly because it gets in the way of an adequate discussion of ideologies and leaves no time 'to explore by-ways'. The undergraduate in the past usually knew how to deal with an official curriculum; he took the initiative on his own account. He knew that being an undergraduate did not mean attending 'courses of lectures', and the universities with the surest traditions never encouraged him in the belief that it did. And in this respect Sir Walter greatly undervalues the examination system, which, as an alternative to the practice of 'getting signed up for attending a course', gives a greatly added freedom to the undergraduate in the disposition of his time and energy, and automatically lessens the evil of an overloaded curriculum. But as usual, Sir Walter wants the moon *and* sixpence: 'obviously the happy-go-lucky system, or absence of system, of mid-Victorian Cambridge can furnish no model for today', but 'it contained an element of great value which...is in danger of being squeezed out.' However, from the point of view of the sort of university we are considering, it may be agreed that an 'overloaded curriculum' is a sign of failure.

The other important point at which a university may be thought to desert its true path is if in its hands the world of learning degenerated into a set of miscellaneous specialisms. This is what Sir Walter believes to have happened. He thinks that each specialism is now explored and taught more efficiently than it used to be, but that virtually no attmept is made to explore the whole to which they belong. I do not think that this is the truth of the matter, and it is disconcerting to find that one of the few efforts the universities have made (in face of considerable pressure in the other direction from the outside) to put a term to this disintegration is attributed to jealousy and laziness: I mean the care usually exercised before a new specialism is allowed to enter the already congested field. Nevertheless, it is undeniable that this disintegration is something we suffer from at the present time and that it is destructive of the sort of university we are considering. And if Sir Walter's remedies

– 'integrating lectures', wider Degree Courses and Combined Honours Schools – are thought to be either wide of the mark or themselves a surrender to disintegration, we should not use his errors to absolve us from considering the matter.

The first thing to be said is that what Sir Walter detects as a flaw in contemporary university education is, in fact, the most difficult of the current problems of philosophy: a century of pretty intense thought has already been given to it without much result. Certainly we should like to see the world of knowledge assume the appearance of unity; but for the present this is one of those things upon which we have to exercise our negative capability. And to expect a university to provide an integration in its curriculum is asking for dishonesty: an integration which sprang merely from an emotional necessity could not fail to be a false, trivial, a worthless formula. And a man who cannot do without certainty in this matter would be better advised to apply his mind in some other direction.

However, on the level of undergraduate education there is something that may be done to relieve the situation. The notion of 'broader-based general degree courses' may be dismissed in this connection; it provides a bogus solution by circumventing the problem. A university should, however, in the first place, select the specialism which it offers for undergraduate study so that there is some chance that each may be seen, even by the undergraduate, as a reflection of the whole. The pressure to provide a technical training for a great variety of professions makes this difficult, but a university of the sort we are considering will disappear unless it is prepared to resist this pressure. The notion that it is somehow illiberal and obscurantist to exercise discrimination in this matter is preposterous. The failure for which the universities may be blamed is not the failure to find and put over a formula to integrate its specialisms, but a failure to be sufficiently selective with regard to the specialisms themselves. Secondly, it is the business of this sort of university to teach at a profound level the various branches of the world of learning which it has chosen to offer to the undergraduate: the real defect of a specialism does not spring from its failure to be the whole, or its failure to know its place in the whole to which it belongs, but when it succeeds in being no more than superficial within its own limits. It would be absurd to expect that every faculty in a university should have the same high standard of excellence or that it should show no variation from time to time in its achievement in this respect. It takes time to acquire a standard of excellence, which is not to be confused with a readiness to keep up to date with the latest items of knowledge and to incorporate them in a syllabus.

The world, which does not understand these things very well, for long enough has been pressing upon the universities, regarded as institutions designed to teach undergraduates, a crux which, unwisely, they have recently shown signs of taking seriously. The question we are asked to decide is, whether the purpose of university education is to acquire knowledge of some specialized branch of learning, connected perhaps with a profession, or whether it is for something else *besides* this. The world will accept the answer that it is for both purposes, but it then wants to know what part of the curriculum is designed to achieve the second purpose; and, in our eagerness to show that we are not doing nothing about it, we begin to talk of 'integrating courses' and of 'culture'. Our real mistake does not lie in a failure to answer the question convincingly, but in the confusion of mind which allows the question to be improperly formulated. The objects of education, it may be said, are to enable a man to make his own thought clear and to attend to what passes before him. The advantage which Antisthenes claimed to have got from philosophy – 'the advantage of being able to converse with myself' – is the chief advantage a man may hope to get from education. These objects, however, are not abstract mental capabilities; to make one's own thoughts clear and to attend to what passes before one is indistinguishable from participating in and handling the civilized inheritance of our society. So far as specific teaching is concerned, our sort of university proposes to achieve these objects by means of the close study of a particular branch of learning. And the ground for this method is the belief that no true and profoundly studied *techne* raises the distinction between acquiring a knowledge of some branch of learning and pursuing the general objects of education. This belief would have less to recommend it if the university were supposed to give a man some sort of final mental equipment or if a particular university were an institute in which only one *techne* was studied; but the university we are considering has never been either of these things. The condition that a *techne* must be 'true' is necessary because there are clearly some specialisms which, the more profoundly they are studied, carry a man further away from the objects of education; the *techne chrematistike* is one of these, and 'culture' is another, and I believe that, if the integration of specialisms assumed the character of a separate *techne*, it would also belong to the class of bogus specialisms; it would be the art of conversation taught to those who had nothing to say. Each 'true' *techne* is, or involves, a particular manner of thinking, and the notion that you can think but without thinking in any particular manner, without reference to some definite universe of discourse, is a philosophical illusion. Every 'true' *techne*, profoundly studied, knows something of its own limits, not because it possesses a comprehensive knowledge of its context and not because it knows everything or has some abstract scheme or key to everything (it cannot have these things while remaining a *techne*), but because it has some insight into its own presuppositions. And when to this is added, as it is added in a university, the presence of other special studies, unless somebody raises the dust, the invitation to conversation is compelling. In short, the problem of intergrating the world of knowledge is a profound and difficult one, but the fact that we do not at the present time see our way through it does not destroy the possibility of a university. The universities have traditions which they may call upon, traditions of discrimination in what they offer for study to undergraduates and traditions of thoroughness of study, and it would be a great mistake to neglect these in favour of an integration generated *ab extra*. The world of knowledge never has been integrated by a *Summa*, and those who urge us to look for it in that direction are unreliable guides whose immoderate thirst has conjured up a mirage.

There was once a building which had been constructed by many hands and over a long period of time. Its architecture represented many different styles, and it so far conflicted with the known rules of construction that it was a matter of wonder that it remained standing. Among its inhabitants were connoisseurs who possessed plans. Some went so far as to claim that their plans were those of the original designer, for in spite of the evidence of their eyes they believed that every building must have an architect. Others among the connoisseurs claimed no more than that their plans represented what the building should have been like. These plans were kept in a room apart and from time to time the collection was added to, some of the additions coming from distant countries. None of the plans bore any noticeable resemblance to the building itself – not because they found every part of it equally convenient or had no projects for improvement, but because they had learned to understand it and to love it. One day a cry of 'Fire' was heard in the building. The connoisseurs ran at once to save their plans; in the building itself they had little interest. It turned out, however, that the fire was, in fact, in a neighbouring bakery and that there was more smoke than flame. But the inhabitants of the bakery fled to the building, and the connoisseurs took the opportunity, while others were extinguishing the fire, to show their plans to the refugees, who, of course, were much interested. They were easily convinced that the building itself was greatly inferior to the plans, and promised the connoisseurs to assist them in the project of demolishing the building (which they had always considered unsightly) and of reconstructing it according to one of the plans. The plan they particularly favoured was one that had recently been received from a remote part of the world.

POLITICAL EDUCATION

1951

The expression 'political education' has fallen on evil days; in the wilful and disingenuous corruption of language which is character-istic of our time it has acquired a sinister meaning. In places other than this, it is associated with that softening of the mind, by force, by alarm, or by the hypnotism of the endless repetition of what was scarcely worth saying once, by means of which whole populations have been reduced to submission. It is, therefore, an enterprise worth undertaking to consider again, in a quiet moment, how we should understand this expression, which joins together two laudable activities, and in doing so plays a small part in rescuing it from abuse.

Politics I take to be the activity of attending to the general arrangements of a set of people whom chance or choice have brought together. In this sense, families, clubs, and learned societies have their 'politics'. But the communities in which this manner of activity is pre-eminent are the hereditary co-operative groups, many of them of ancient lineage, all of them aware of a

Author's note: First delivered as an Inaugural Lecture at the London School of Economics, this piece was commented upon from various points of view. The notes I have now added, and a few changes I have made in the text, are designed to remove some of the misunderstandings it provoked. But, in general, the reader is advised to remember that it is concerned with understanding and explaining political activity which, in my view, is the proper object of political education. What people project in political activity, and different styles of political conduct, are considered here, first merely because they sometimes reveal the way in which political activity is being understood, and secondly because it is commonly (though I think wrongly) supposed that explanations are warrants for conduct.

past, a present, and a future, which we call 'states'. For most people, political activity is a secondary activity – that is to say, they have something else to do besides attending to these arrangements. But, as we have come to understand it, the activity is one in which every member of the group who is neither a child nor a lunatic has some part and some responsibility. With us it is, at one level or another, a universal activity.

I speak of this activity as 'attending to arrangements', rather than as 'making arrangements', because in these hereditary co-operative groups the activity is never offered the blank sheet of infinite possibility. In any generation, even the most revolutionary, the arrangements which are enjoyed always far exceed those which are recognized to stand in need of attention, and those which are being prepared for enjoyment are few in comparison with those which receive amendment: the new is an insignificant proportion of the whole. There are some people, of course, who allow themselves to speak

> *As if arrangements were intended*
> *For nothing else but to be mended,*

but for most of us, our determination to improve our conduct does not prevent us from recognizing that the greater part of what we have is not a burden to be carried or an incubus to be thrown off, but an inheritance to be enjoyed. And a certain degree of shabbiness is joined with every real convenience.

Now, attending to the arrangements of a society is an activity which, like every other, has to be learned. Politics make a call upon knowledge. Consequently, it is not irrelevant to inquire into the kind of knowledge which is involved, and to investigate the nature of political education. I do not, however, propose to ask what information we should equip ourselves with before we begin to be politically active, or what we need to know in order to be successful politicians, but to inquire into the kind of knowledge we unavoidably call upon whenever we are engaged in political activity and to get from this an understanding of the nature of political education.

Our thoughts on political education, then, might be supposed to spring from our understanding of political activity and the kind of knowledge it involves. And it would appear that what is wanted at this point is a definition of political activity from which to draw some conclusions. But this, I think, would be a mistaken way of going about our business. What we require is not so much a definition of politics from which to deduce the character of political education, as an understanding of political activity which includes a recognition of the sort of education it involves. For, to understand an activity is to know it as a concrete whole; it is to recognize the activity as having the source of its movement within itself. An understanding which leaves the activity in debt to something out-side itself is, for that reason, an inadequate understanding. And if political activity is impossible without a certain kind of knowledge and a certain sort of education, then this knowledge and education are not mere appendages to the activity but are part of the activity itself and must be incorporated in our understanding of it. We should not, therefore, seek a definition of politics in order to deduce from it the character of political knowledge and education, but rather observe the kind of knowledge and education which is in-herent in any understanding of political activity, and use this observation as a means of improving our understanding of politics.

My proposal, then, is to consider the adequacy of two current understandings of politics, together with the sort of knowledge and kind of education they imply, and by improving upon them to reach what may perhaps be a more adequate understanding at once of political activity itself and the knowledge and education which belongs to it.

2

In the understanding of some people, politics is what may be called an empirical activity. Attending to the arrangements of a society is waking up each morning and considering 'What would I like to do?' or 'What would somebody else (whom I desire to please) like to see done?' and doing it. This understanding of political activity may be called politics without a policy. On the briefest inspection it will appear a concept of politics difficult to substantiate; it does not look like a possible manner of activity at all. But a near approach to it is, perhaps, to be detected in the politics of the pro-verbial oriental despot, or in the politics of the wall-scribbler and the vote-catcher. And the result may be supposed to be chaos modified by whatever consistency is allowed to creep into caprice. They are the politics attributed to the first Lord Liverpool, of whom Acton said, 'The secret of his policy was that he had none', and of whom a Frenchman remarked that if he had been present at the creation of the world he would have said, *'Mon Dieu, conservons le chaos'*. It seems, then, that a concrete activity, which may be de-scribed as an approximation to empirical politics, is possible. But it is clear that, although knowledge of a sort belongs to this style of political activity (knowledge, as the French say, not of ourselves but only of our appetites), the only kind of education appropriate to it would be an education in lunacy – learning to be ruled solely by passing desires. And this reveals the important point: namely, that to understand politics as a purely empirical activity is to misunderstand it, because empiricism by itself is not a concrete manner of activity at all, and can become a partner in a concrete manner of activity only when it is joined with something else – in science, for example, when it is joined with hypothesis. What is significant about this understanding of politics is not that some sort of approach to it can appear, but that it mistakes for a concrete, self-moved manner of activity what is never more than an abstract moment in any manner of being active. Of course, politics is the pursuit of what is desired and of what is desired at the moment; but precisely because they are this, they can never be the pursuit of merely what recommends itself from moment to moment. The activity of desiring does not take this course; caprice is never absolute. From a practical point of view, then, we may decry the *style* of politics which approximates to pure empiricism because we can observe in it an approach to lunacy. But from a theoretical point of view, purely empirical politics are not something difficult to achieve or proper to be avoided, they are merely impossible; the product of a misunderstanding.

3

The understanding of politics as an empirical activity is, then, inadequate because it fails to reveal a concrete manner of activity at all. And it has the incidental defect of seeming to encourage the thoughtless to pursue a *style* of attending to the arrangements of their society which is likely to have unfortunate results; to try to do something which is inherently impossible is always a corrupting enterprise. We must, if we can, improve upon it. And the impulse to improve may be given a direction by asking, 'What is it that this understanding of politics has neglected to observe?' What (to put it crudely) has it left out which, if added in, would compose an understanding in which politics are revealed as a self-moved (or concrete) manner of activity? And the answer to the question is, or seems to be, available as soon as the question is formulated. It would appear that what this understanding of politics lacks is something to set empiricism to work, something to correspond with specific hypothesis in science, an end to be pursued that is more extensive than a merely instant desire. And this, it should be observed, is not merely a good companion for empiricism; it is something without which empiricism in action is impossible. Let us explore this suggestion, and in order to bring it to a point I will state it in the form of a proposition: that politics appear as a self-moved manner of activity when empiricism is preceded and guided by an ideological activity. I am not concerned with the so-called ideological *style* of politics as a desirable or undesirable manner of attending to the arrangements of a society; I am concerned only with the contention that when to the ineluctable element of empiricism (doing what one wants to do) is added a political ideology, a self-moved manner of activity appears, and that consequently this may be regarded in principle as an adequate understanding of political activity.

As I understand it, a political ideology purports to be an abstract principle, or a set of related abstract principles, which has been independently premeditated. It supplies in advance of the activity of attending to the arrangements of a society a formulated end to be pursued, and in so doing it provides a means of distinguishing between those desires which ought to be encouraged and those which ought to be suppressed or redirected.

The simplest sort of political ideology is a single abstract idea, such as Freedom, Equality, Maximum Productivity, Racial Purity, or Happiness. And in that case political activity is understood as the enterprise of seeing that the arrangements of a society conform to or reflect the chosen abstract idea. It is usual, however, to recognize the need for a complex scheme of related ideas, rather than a single idea, and the examples pointed to will be such systems of ideas as: 'the principles of 1789', 'Liberalism', 'Democracy', 'Marxism', or the Atlantic Charter. These principles need not be considered absolute or immune from change (though they are frequently so considered), but their value lies in their having been premeditated. They compose an understanding of *what* is to be pursued independent of *how* it is to be pursued. A political ideology purports to supply in advance knowledge of what 'Freedom' or 'Democracy' or 'Justice' is, and in this manner sets empiricism to work. Such a set of principles is, of course, capable of being argued about and reflected upon; it is something that men compose for themselves, and they may later remember it or write it down. But the condition upon which it can perform the service assigned to it is that it owes nothing to the activity it controls. 'To know the true good of the community is what constitutes the science of legislation', said Bentham; 'the art consists in finding the means to realize that good'. The contention that we have before us, then, is that empiricism can be set to work (and a concrete, self-moved manner of activity appear) when there is added to it a guide of this sort: desire and something not generated by desire.

Now, there is no doubt about the sort of knowledge which political activity, understood in this manner, calls upon. What is required, in the first place, is knowledge of the chosen political ideology – a knowledge of the ends to be pursued, a knowledge of what we want to do. Of course, if we are to be successful in pursuing these ends we shall need knowledge of another sort also – a knowledge, shall we say, of economics and psychology. But the common characteristic of all the kinds of knowledge required is that they may be, and should be, gathered in advance of the activity of attending to the arrangements of a society. Moreover, the appropriate sort of education will be an education in which the chosen political ideology is taught and learned, in which the techniques necessary for success are acquired, and (if we are so unfortunate as to find ourselves empty-handed in the matter of an ideology) an education in the skill of abstract thought and premeditation necessary to compose one for ourselves. The education we shall need is one which enables us to expound, defend, implement, and possibly invent a political ideology.

In casting around for some convincing demonstration that this understanding of politics reveals a self-moved manner of activity, we should no doubt consider ourselves rewarded if we could find an example of politics being conducted precisely in this manner. This at least would constitute a sign that we were on the right track. The defect, it will be remembered, of the understanding of politics as a purely empirical activity was that it revealed, not a manner of activity at all, but an abstraction; and this defect made itself manifest in our inability to find a *style* of politics which was anything more than an approximation to it. How does the understanding of politics as empiricism joined with an ideology fare in this respect? And without being over-confident, we may perhaps think that this is where we wade ashore. For we would appear to be in no difficulty whatever in finding an example of political activity which corresponds to this understanding of it: half the world, at a conservative estimate, seems to conduct its affairs in precisely this manner. And further, is it not so manifestly a possible style of politics that, even if we disagree with a particular ideology, we find nothing technically absurd in the writings of those who urge it upon us as an admirable style of politics? At least its advocates seem to know what they are talking about: they understand not only the manner of the activity but also the sort of knowledge and the kind of education it involves. 'Every schoolboy in Russia', wrote Sir Norman Angel, 'is familiar with the doctrine of Marx and can write its catechism. How many British schoolboys have any corresponding knowledge of the principles enunciated by Mill in his incomparable essay on Liberty?' 'Few people', says Mr. E. H. Carr, 'any longer contest the thesis that the child should be educated *in* the official ideology of his country.' In short, if we are looking for a sign to indicate that the understanding of politics as empirical activity preceded by ideological activity is an adequate understanding, we can scarcely be mistaken in supposing that we have it to hand.

And yet there is perhaps room for doubt: doubt first of all whether in principle this understanding of politics reveals a self-moved manner of activity; and doubt, consequentially, whether what have been identified as examples of a *style* of politics corresponding exactly to this understanding have been properly identified.

The contention we are investigating is that attending to the arrangements of a society can begin with a premeditated ideology, can begin with independently acquired knowledge of the ends to be pursued.[1] It is supposed that a political ideology is the product of intellectual premeditation and that, because it is a body of principles not itself in debt to the activity of attending to the arrangements of society, it is able to determine and guide the direction of that activity. If, however, we consider more closely the character of a political ideology, we find at once that this supposition is falsified. So far from a political ideology being the quasi-divine parent of political activity, it turns out to be its earthly stepchild. Instead of an independently premeditated scheme of ends to be pursued, it is a system of ideas abstracted from the manner in which people have been accustomed to go about the business of attending to the arrangements of their societies. The pedigree of every political ideology shows it to be the creature, not of premeditation in advance of political activity, but of meditation upon a manner of politics. In short, political activity comes first and a political ideology follows after; and the understanding of politics we are investigating has the disadvantage of being, in the strict sense, preposterous.

Let us consider the matter first in relation to scientific hypothesis, which I have taken to play a role in scientific activity in some re-

---

[1] This is the case, for example, with Natural Law; whether it is taken to be an explanation of political activity or, improperly, as a guide to political conduct.

spects similar to that of an ideology in politics. If a scientific hypothesis were a self-generated bright idea which owed nothing to
scientific activity, then empiricism governed by hypothesis could
be considered to compose a self-contained manner of activity; but
this certainly is not its character. The truth is that only a man who
is already a scientist can formulate a scientific hypothesis; that is,
an hypothesis is not an independent invention capable of guiding
scientific inquiry, but a dependent supposition which arises as an
abstraction from within already existing scientific activity. Moreover, even when the specific hypothesis has in this manner been
formulated, it is inoperative as a guide to research without
constant reference to the traditions of scientific inquiry from which
it was abstracted. The concrete situation does not appear until the
specific hypothesis, which is the occasion of empiricism being set to
work, is recognized as itself the creature of knowing how to conduct
a scientific inquiry.

Or consider the example of cookery. It might be supposed that
an ignorant man, some edible materials, and a cookery book compose together the necessities of a self-moved (or concrete) activity
called cooking. But nothing is further from the truth. The cookery
book is not an independently generated beginning from which
cooking can spring; it is nothing more than an abstract of somebody's knowledge of how to cook: it is the stepchild, not the parent
of the activity. The book, in its turn, may help to set a man on to
dressing a dinner, but if it were his sole guide he could never, in
fact, begin: the book speaks only to those who know already the
kind of thing to expect from it and consequently how to interpret it.

Now, just as a cookery book presupposes somebody who knows
how to cook, and its use presupposes somebody who already knows
how to use it, and just as a scientific hypothesis springs from a knowledge of how to conduct a scientific investigation and separated
from that knowledge is powerless to set empiricism profitably to
work, so a political ideology must be understood, not as an independently premeditated beginning for political activity, but as
knowledge (abstract and generalized) of a concrete manner of
attending to the arrangements of a society. The catechism which
sets out the purposes to be pursued merely abridges a concrete
manner of behaviour in which those purposes are already hidden.
It does not exist in advance of political activity, and by itself it is
always an insufficient guide. Political enterprises, the ends to be
pursued, the arrangements to be established (all the normal
ingredients of a political ideology), cannot be premeditated in
advance of a manner of attending to the arrangements of a society;

what we do, and moreover what we want to do, is the creature of *how* we are accustomed to conduct our affairs. Indeed, it often reflects no more than a discovered ability to do something which is then translated into an authority to do it.

On 4 August 1789, for the complex and bankrupt social and political system of France was substituted the Rights of Man. Reading this document we come to the conclusion that somebody has done some thinking. Here, displayed in a few sentences, is a political ideology: a system of rights and duties, a scheme of ends – justice, freedom, equality, security, property and the rest – ready and waiting to be put into practice for the first time. 'For the first time?' Not a bit of it. This ideology no more existed in advance of political practice than a cookery book exists in advance of knowing how to cook. Certainly it was the product of somebody's reflection, but it was not the product of reflection in advance of political activity. For here, in fact, are disclosed, abstracted and abridged, the common law rights of Englishmen, the gift not of independent premeditation or divine munificence, but of centuries of the day-to-day attending to the arrangements of an historic society. Or consider Locke's *Second Treatise of Civil Government*, read in America and in France in the eighteenth century as a statement of abstract principles to be put into practice, regarded there as a preface to political activity. But so far from being a preface, it has all the marks of a postscript, and its power to guide derived from its roots in actual political experience. Here, set down in abstract terms, is a brief conspectus of the manner in which Englishmen were accustomed to go about the business of attending to their arrangements – a brilliant abridgement of the political habits of Englishmen. Or consider this passage from a contemporary continental writer: 'Freedom keeps Europeans in unrest and movement. They wish to have freedom, and at the same time they know they have not got it.' And having established the end to be pursued, political activity is represented as the realization of this end. But the 'freedom' which can be pursued is not an independently premeditated 'ideal' or a dream; like scientific hypothesis, it is something which is already intimated in a concrete manner of behaving. Freedom, like a recipe for game pie, is not a bright idea; it is not a 'human right' to be deduced from some speculative concept of human nature. The freedom which we enjoy is nothing more than arrangements, procedures of a certain kind: the freedom of an Englishman is not something exemplified in the procedure of *habeas corpus*, it *is*, at that point, the availability of that procedure. And the freedom which we wish to enjoy is not an 'ideal' which we premeditate independently of our political experience; it is what is already intimated in that experience.[2]

On this reading, then, the systems of abstract ideas we call 'ideologies' are abstracts of some kind of concrete activity. Most political ideologies, and certainly the most useful of them (because they unquestionably have their use), are abstracts of the political traditions of some society. But it sometimes happens that an ideology is offered as a guide to politics which is an abstract, not of political experience, but of some other manner of activity – war, religion, or the conduct of industry, for example. And here the model we are shown is not only abstract, but is also inappropriate on account of the irrelevance of the activity from which it has been abstracted. This, I think, is one of the defects of the model provided by the Marxist ideology. But the important point is that, at most, an ideology is an abbreviation of some manner of concrete activity.

We are now, perhaps, in a position to perceive more accurately the character of what may be called the ideological *style* of politics, and to observe that its existence offers no ground for supposing that the understanding of political activity as empiricism guided solely by an ideology is an adequate understanding. The ideological style of politics is a confused style. Properly speaking, it is a traditional manner of attending to the arrangements of a society which has been abridged into a doctrine of ends to be pursued, the abridgement (together with the necessary technical knowledge) being erroneously regarded as the sole guide relied upon. In certain circumstances an abridgement of this kind may be valuable; it gives sharpness of outline and precision to a political tradition which the occasion may make seem appropriate. When a manner of attending to arrangements is to be transplanted from the society in which it has grown up into another society (always a questionable enterprise), the simplification of an ideology may appear as an asset. If, for example, the English manner of politics is to be planted elsewhere in the world, it is perhaps appropriate that it should first be abridged into something called 'democracy' before it is packed up and shipped abroad. There is, of course, an alternative method: the method by which what is exported is the detail and not the abridgement of the tradition, and the workmen travel with the tools – the method which made the British Empire. But it is a slow and costly method. And, particularly with men in a

---

[2] Cf. 'Substantive law has the first look of being gradually secreted in the interstices of procedure.' Sir Henry Maine, *Dissertations on Early Law and Custom* (London: John Murray, 1883).

hurry, *l'homme à programme* with his abridgement wins every time; his slogans enchant, while the resident magistrate is seen only as a sign of servility. But whatever the apparent appropriateness on occasion of the ideological style of politics, the defect of the explanation of political activity connected with it becomes apparent when we consider the sort of knowledge and the kind of education it encourages us to believe is sufficient for understanding the activity of attending to the arrangements of a society. For it suggests that a knowledge of the chosen political ideology can take the place of understanding a tradition of political behaviour. The wand and the book come to be regarded as themselves potent, and not merely the symbols of potency. The arrangements of a society are made to appear, not as manners of behaviour, but as pieces of machinery to be transported about the world indiscriminately. The complexities of the tradition which have been squeezed out in the process of abridgement are taken to be unimportant: 'the rights of man' are understood to exist insulated from a manner of attending to arrangements. And because, in practice, the abridgement is never by itself a sufficient guide, we are encouraged to fill it out, not with our suspect political experience, but with experience drawn from other (often irrelevant) concretely understood activities, such as war, the conduct of industry, or Trade Union negotiation.

4

The understanding of politics as the activity of attending to the arrangements of a society under the guidance of an independently premeditated ideology is, then, no less a misunderstanding than the understanding of it as a purely empirical activity. Wherever else politics may begin, they cannot begin in ideological activity. And in an attempt to improve upon this understanding of politics, we have already observed in principle what needs to be recognized in order to have an intelligible concept. Just as scientific hypothesis cannot appear, and is impossible to operate, except within an already existing tradition of scientific investigation, so a scheme of ends for political activity appears within, and can be evaluated only when it is related to an already existing tradition of how to attend to our arrangements. In politics, the only concrete manner of activity detectable is one in which empiricism and the ends to be pursued are recognized as dependent, alike for their existence and their operation, upon a traditional manner of behaviour.

Politics is the activity of attending to the general arrangements of a collection of people who, in respect of their common recognition of a manner of attending to its arrangements, compose a single community. To suppose a collection of people without recognized traditions of behaviour, or one which enjoyed arrangements which intimated no direction for change and needed no attention,[3] is to suppose a people incapable of politics.

This activity, then, springs neither from instant desires, nor from general principles, but from the existing traditions of behaviour themselves. And the form it takes, because it can take no other, is the amendment of existing arrangements by exploring and pursuing what is intimated in them. The arrangements which constitute a society capable of political activity, whether they are customs or institutions or laws or diplomatic decisions, are at once coherent and incoherent; they compose a pattern and at the same time they intimate a sympathy for what does not fully appear. Political activity is the exploration of that sympathy; and consequently, relevant political reasoning will be the convincing exposure of a sympathy, present but not yet followed up, and the convincing demonstration that now is the appropriate moment for recognizing it. For example, the legal status of women in our society was for a long time (and perhaps still is) in comparative confusion, because the rights and duties which composed it intimated rights and duties which were nevertheless not recognized. And, on the view of things I am suggesting, the only cogent reason to be advanced for the technical 'enfranchisement' of women was that in all or most other important respects they had already been enfranchised. Arguments drawn from abstract natural right, from 'justice', or from some general concept of feminine personality, must be regarded as either irrelevant, or as unfortunately disguised forms of the one valid argument: namely, that there was an incoherence in the arrangements of the society which pressed convincingly for remedy. In politics, then, every enterprise is a consequential enterprise, the pursuit, not of a dream, nor of a general principle, but of an intimation.[4] What we have to make do with is something less imposing than logical implications or necessary consequences; but if the intimations of a tradition of behaviour are less dignified or more elusive than these, they are not on that account less important. Of course, there is no piece of mistake-proof apparatus by means of which we can elicit the intimation most worthwhile

---

[3] For example, a society in which law was believed to be a divine gift.
[4] See terminal note, p. 155.

pursuing; and not only do we often make gross errors of judgement in this matter, but also the total effect of a desire satisfied is so little to be forecast that our activity of amendment is often found to lead us where we would not go. Moreover, the whole enterprise is liable at any moment to be perverted by the incursion of an approximation to empiricism in the pursuit of power. These are features which can never be eliminated; they belong to the character of political activity. But it may be believed that our mistakes of understanding will be less frequent and less disastrous if we escape the illusion that politics is ever anything more than the pursuit of intimations; a conversation, not an argument.

Now, every society which is intellectually alive is liable, from time to time, to abridge its tradition of behaviour into a scheme of abstract ideas; and on occasion political discussion will be concerned, not (like the debates in the *Iliad*) with isolated transactions, nor (like the speeches in Thucydides) with policies and traditions of activity, but with general principles. And in this there is no harm; perhaps even some positive benefit. It is possible that the distorting mirror of an ideology will reveal important hidden passages in the tradition, as a caricature reveals the potentialities of a face; and if this is so, the intellectual enterprise of seeing what a tradition looks like when it is reduced to an ideology will be a useful part of political education. But to make use of abridgement as a technique for exploring the intimations of a political tradition, to use it, that is, as a scientist uses hypothesis, is one thing; it is something different, and something inappropriate, to understand political activity itself as the activity of amending the arrangements of a society to make them agree with the provisions of an ideology. For then a character has been attributed to an ideology which it is unable to sustain, and we may find ourselves, in practice, directed by a false and a misleading guide: false, because in the abridgement, however skillfully it has been performed, a single intimation is apt to be exaggerated and proposed for unconditional pursuit, and the benefit to be had from observing what the distortion reveals is lost when the distortion itself is given the office of a criterion; misleading, because the abridgement itself never, in fact, provides the whole of the knowledge used in political activity.

There will be some people who, though in general agreement with this understanding of political activity, will suspect that it confuses what is, perhaps, normal with what is necessary, and that important exceptions (of great contemporary relevance) have been lost in a hazy generality. It is all very well, it may be said, to observe in politics the activity of exploring and pursuing the intimations of a tradition of behaviour, but what light does this throw upon a political crisis such as the Norman Conquest of England, or the establishment of the Soviet regime in Russia? It would be foolish, of course, to deny the possibility of serious political crisis. But if we exclude (as we must) a genuine cataclysm which for the time being made an end of politics by altogether obliterating a current tradition of behaviour (which is *not* what happened in Anglo-Saxon England or in Russia),[5] there is little to support the view that even the most serious political upheaval carries us outside this understanding of politics. A tradition of behaviour is not a fixed and inflexible manner of doing things; it is a flow of sympathy. It may be temporarily disrupted by the incursion of a foreign influence, it may be diverted, restricted, arrested, or become dried up, and it may reveal so deep-seated an incoherence that (even without foreign assistance) a crisis appears. And if, in order to meet these crises, there were some steady, unchanging, independent guide to which a society might resort, it would no doubt be well advised to do so. But no such guide exists; we have no resources outside the fragments, the vestiges, the relics of its own tradition of behaviour which the crisis has left untouched. For even the help we may get from the traditions of another society (or from a tradition of a vaguer sort which is shared by a number of societies) is conditional upon our being able to assimilate them to our own arrangements and our own manner of attending to our arrangements. The hungry and helpless man is mistaken if he supposes that he overcomes the crisis by means of a tin-opener: what saves him is somebody else's knowledge of how to cook, which he can make use of only because he is not himself entirely ignorant. In short, political crisis (even when it seems to be imposed upon a society by changes beyond its control) always appears *within* a tradition of political activity; and 'salvation' comes from the unimpaired resources of the tradition itself. Those societies which retain, in changing circumstances, a lively sense of their own identity and continuity (which are without that hatred of their own experiences which makes them desire to efface it) are to be counted fortunate, not because they possess what others lack, but because they have already mobilized what none is without and all, in fact, rely upon.

In political activity, then, men sail a boundless and bottomless

[5] The Russian Revolution (what actually happened in Russia) was not the implementation of an abstract design worked out by Lenin and others in Switzerland: it was a modification of *Russian* circumstances. And the French Revolution was far more closely connected with the *ancien régime* than with Locke or America.

sea; there is neither harbour for shelter nor floor for anchorage, neither starting-place nor appointed destination. The enterprise is to keep afloat on an even keel; the sea is both friend and enemy; and the seamanship consists in using the resources of a traditional manner of behaviour in order to make a friend of every hostile occasion.[6]

A depressing doctrine, it will be said – even by those who do not make the mistake of adding in an element of crude determinism which, in fact, it has no place for. A tradition of behaviour is not a groove within which we are destined to grind out our helpless and unsatisfying lives: *Spartam nactus es; hanc exorna*. But in the main the depression springs from the exclusion of hopes that were false and the discovery that guides, reputed to be of superhuman wisdom and skill are, in fact, of a somewhat different character. If the doctrine deprives us of a model laid up in heaven to which we should approximate our behaviour, at least it does not lead us into a morass where every choice is equally good or equally to be deplored. And if it suggests that politics are *nur für die Schwindelfreie*, that should depress only those who have lost their nerve.

5

The sin of the academic is that he takes so long in coming to the point. Nevertheless, there is some virtue in his dilatoriness; what he has to offer may, in the end, be no great matter, but at least it is not unripe fruit, and to pluck it is the work of a moment. We set out to consider the kind of knowledge involved in political activity and the appropriate sort of education. And if the understanding of politics I have recommended is not a misunderstanding, there is little doubt about the kind of knowledge and the sort of education which belongs to it. It is knowledge, as profound as we can make it, of our tradition of political behaviour. Other knowledge, certainly, is

---

[6] To those who seem to themselves to have a clear view of an immediate destination (that is, of a condition of human circumstance to be achieved), and who are confident that this condition is proper to be imposed upon everybody, this will seem an unduly sceptical understanding of political activity; but they may be asked where they have got it from, and whether they imagine that 'political activity' will come to an end with the achievement of this condition? And if they agree that some more distant destination may then be expected to disclose itself, does not this situation entail an understanding of politics as an open-ended activity such as I have described? Or do they understand politics as making the necessary arrangements for a set of castaways who have always in reserve the thought that they are going to be 'rescued'?

desirable in addition; but this is the knowledge without which we cannot make use of whatever else we may have learned.

A tradition of behaviour is a tricky thing to get to know. Indeed, it may even appear to be essentially unintelligible. It is neither fixed nor finished; it has no changeless centre to which understanding can anchor itself; there is no sovereign purpose to be perceived or invariable direction to be detected; there is no model to be copied, idea to be realized, or rule to be followed. Some parts of it may change more slowly than others, but none is immune from change. Everything is temporary. Nevertheless, though a tradition of behaviour is flimsy and elusive, it is not without identity, and what makes it a possible object of knowledge is the fact that all its parts do not change at the same time and that the changes it undergoes are potential within it. Its principle is a principle of *continuity*: authority is diffused between past, present, and future; between the old, the new, and what is to come. It is steady because, though it moves, it is never wholly in motion; and though it is tranquil, it is never wholly at rest.[7] Nothing that ever belonged to it is completely lost; we are always swerving back to recover and to make something topical out of even its remotest moments; and nothing for long remains unmodified. Everything is temporary, but nothing is arbitrary. Everything figures by comparison, not with what stands next to it, but with the whole. And since a tradition of behaviour is not susceptible of the distinction between essence and accident, knowledge of it is unavoidably knowledge of its detail: to know only the gist is to know nothing. What has to be learned is not an abstract idea, or a set of tricks, not even a ritual, but a concrete, coherent manner of living in all its intricacy.

It is clear, then, that we must not entertain the hope of acquiring this difficult understanding by easy methods. Though the knowledge we seek is municipal, not universal, there is no short cut to it. Moreover, political education is not merely a matter of coming to understand a tradition, it is learning how to participate in a conversation: it is at once initiation into an inheritance in which we have a life interest, and the exploration of its intimations. There will always remain something of a mystery about how a tradition of political behaviour is learned, and perhaps the only certainly is that there is no point at which learning it can properly be said to begin. The politics of a community are not less individual (and not

---

[7] The critic who found 'some mystical qualities' in this passage leaves me puzzled: it seems to me an exceedingly matter-of-fact description of the characteristics of any tradition – the Common Law of England, for example, the so-called British Constitution, the Christian religion, modern physics, the game of cricket, shipbuilding.

more so) than its language, and they are learned and practised in the same manner. We do not begin to learn our native language by learning the alphabet, or by learning its grammar; we do not begin by learning words, but words in use; we do not begin (as we begin in reading) with what is easy and go on to what is more difficult; we do not begin at school, but in the cradle; and what we say springs always from our manner of speaking. And this is true also of our political education: it begins in the enjoyment of a tradition, in the observation and imitation of the behaviour of our elders, and there is little or nothing in the world which comes before us as we open our eyes which does not contribute to it. We are aware of a past and a future as soon as we are aware of a present. Long before we are of an age to take interest in a book about our politics we are acquiring that complex and intricate knowledge of our political tradition without which we could not make sense of a book when we come to open it. And the projects we entertain are the creatures of our tradition. The greater part, then – perhaps the important part – of our political education we acquire haphazardly in finding our way about the natural-artificial world into which we are born, and there is no other way of acquiring it. There will, of course, be more to acquire, and it will be more readily acquired if we have the good fortune to be born into a rich and lively political tradition and among those who are well educated politically; the lineaments of political activity will earlier become distinct: but even the most needy society and the most cramped surroundings have some political education to offer, and we take what we can get.

But if this is the manner of our beginning, there are deeper recesses to explore. Politics is a proper subject for academic study; there is something to think about and it is important that we should think about the appropriate things. Here also, and everywhere, the governing consideration is that what we are learning to understand is a political tradition, a concrete manner of behaviour. And for this reason it is proper that, at the academic level, the study of politics should be an historical study – not, in the first place, because it is proper to be concerned with the past, but because we need to be concerned with the detail of the concrete. It is true that nothing appears on the present surface of a tradition of political activity which has not its roots deep in the past, and that not to observe it coming into being is often to be denied the clue to its significance; and for this reason genuine historical study is an indispensable part of a political education. But what is equally important is not what happened, here or there, but what people have thought and said about what happened: the history, not of political ideas, but of the manner of our political thinking. Every society, by the underlinings it makes in the book of its history, constructs a legend of its own fortunes which it keeps up to date and in which is hidden its own understanding of its politics; and the historical investigation of this legend – not to expose its errors but to understand its prejudices – must be a pre-eminent part of a political education. It is, then, in the study of genuine history, and of this quasi-history which reveals in its backward glances the tendencies which are afoot, that we may hope to escape one of the most insidious current misunderstandings of political activity – the misunderstanding in which institutions and procedures appear as pieces of machinery designed to achieve a purpose settled in advance, instead of as manners of behaviour which are meaningless when separated from their context: the misunderstanding, for example, in which Mill convinced himself that something called 'Representative Government' was a 'form' of politics which could be regarded as proper to any society which had reached a certain level of what is called 'civilization'; in short, the misunderstanding in which we regard our arrangements and institutions as something more significant than the footprints of thinkers and statesmen who knew which way to turn their feet without knowing anything about a final destination.

Nevertheless, to be concerned only with one's own tradition of political activity is not enough. A political education worth the name must embrace, also, knowledge of the politics of other contemporary societies. It must do this because some at least of our political activity is related to that of other people's, and not to know how they go about attending to their own arrangements is not to know the course they will pursue and not to know what resources to call upon in our own tradition; and because to know only one's own tradition is not to know even that. But here again two observations must be made. We did not begin yesterday to have relations with our neighbours; and we do not require constantly to be hunting outside the tradition of our politics to find some special formula or some merely *ad hoc* expedient to direct those relations. It is only when wilfully or negligently we forget the resources of understanding and initiative which belong to our tradition that, like actors who have forgotten their part, we are obliged to gag. And secondly, the only knowledge worth having about the politics of another society is the same kind of knowledge as we seek of our own tradition. Here also, *la verité reste dans les nuances*; and a comparative study of institutions, for example, which obscured this would provide only an illusory sense of having understood what nevertheless remains a secret. The study of another people's politics, like a study of our own, should be an ecological study of a tradition of behaviour, not an anatomical study of mechanical devices or the investigation of an ideology. And only when our study is of this sort shall we find ourselves in the way of being stimulated, but not intoxicated, by the manners of others. To range the world in order to select the 'best' of the practices and purposes of others (as the eclectic Zeuxis is said to have tried to compose a figure more beautiful than Helen's by putting together features each notable for its perfection) is a corrupting enterprise and one of the surest ways of losing one's political balance; but to investigate the concrete manner in which another people goes about the business of attending to its arrangements may reveal significant passages in our own tradition which might otherwise remain hidden.

There is a third department in the academic study of politics which must be considered – what, for want of a better name, I shall call a philosophical study. Reflection on political activity may take place at various levels: we may consider what resources our political tradition offers for dealing with a certain situation, or we may abridge our political experience into a doctrine, which may be used, as a scientist uses a hypothesis, to explore its intimations. But beyond these, and other manners of political thinking, there is a range of reflection, the object of which is to consider the place of political activity itself on the map of our total experience. Reflection of this sort has gone on in every society which is politically conscious and intellectually alive; and so far as European societies are concerned, the inquiry has uncovered a variety of intellectual problems which each generation has formulated in its own way and has tackled with the technical resources at its disposal. And because political philosophy is not what may be called a 'progressive' science, accumulating solid results and reaching conclusions upon which further investigation may be based with confidence, its history is especially important: indeed, in a sense, it has nothing but a history, which is a history of the incoherencies philosophers have detected in common ways of thinking and the manner of solution they have proposed, rather than a history of doctrines and systems. The study of this history may be supposed to have a considerable place in a political education, and the enterprise of understanding the turn which contemporary reflection has given to it, an even more considerable place. Political philosophy cannot be expected to increase our ability to be successful in political activity. It will not help us to distinguish between good and bad political projects; it has no power to guide or to direct us in the enterprise of pursuing the intimations of our tradition. But the patient analysis of the general ideas which have come to be connected with political activity – ideas such as nature, artifice, reason, will, law, authority and obligation – in so far as it succeeds in removing some of the crookedness from our thinking and leads to a more economical use of concepts, is an activity neither to be overrated nor despised. But it must be understood as an explanatory, not a practical, activity, and if we pursue it, we may hope only to be less often cheated by ambiguous statement and irrelevant argument.

Abeunt studia in mores. The fruits of a political education will appear in the manner in which we think and speak about politics and perhaps in the manner in which we conduct our political activity. To select items from this prospective harvest must always be hazardous, and opinions will differ about what is most important. But for myself I should hope for two things. The more profound our understanding of political activity, the less we shall be at the mercy of a plausible but mistaken analogy, the less we shall be tempted by a false or irrelevant model. And the more thoroughly we understand our own political tradition, the more readily its whole resources are available to us, the less likely we shall be to embrace the illusions which wait for the ignorant and the unwary: the illusion that in politics we can get on without a tradition of behaviour, the illusion that the abridgement of a tradition is itself a sufficient guide, and the illusion that in politics there is anywhere a safe harbour, a destination to be reached or even a detectable strand of progress. 'The world is the best of all possible worlds, and *everything* in it is a necessary evil.'

The Pursuit of Intimations

1. This expression, as I hoped I had made clear, was intended as a description of what political activity actually is in the circumstances indicated, namely, in the 'hereditary, co-operative groups, many of them of ancient lineage, all of them aware of a past, a present, and a future, which we call "states"'. Critics who find this to be so specialized a description that it fails altogether to account for some of the most significant passages in modern political history are, or course, making a relevant comment. But those who find this expression to be meaningless in respect of every so-called 'revolutionary' situation and every essay in so-called 'idealistic'

politics may be asked to think again, remembering that it is neither intended as a description of the motives of politicians nor of what they believe themselves to be doing, but of what they actually succeed in doing.

I connected with this understanding of political activity two further propositions: first, that if true, it must be supposed to have some bearing upon how we study politics, that is, upon political education; secondly, that if true, it may be supposed to have some bearing upon how we conduct ourselves in political activity – there being, perhaps, some advantage in thinking and speaking and arguing in a manner consonant with what we are really doing. The second of these propositions I do not think to be very important.

2. It has been concluded that this understanding of political activity reduces it to 'acting on hunches', 'following intuitions' and that it 'discourages argument of any sort'. Nothing I have said warrants this conclusion. The conclusion I myself drew in this connection was that, if this understanding of political activity were true, certain forms of argument (for example, arguments designed to determine the correspondence of a political proposal with Natural Law or with abstract 'justice') must be considered either irrelevant or as clumsy formulations of other and relevant inquiries, and must be understood to have a merely rhetorical or persuasive value.

3. It has been suggested that this understanding of political activity provides no standard or criterion for distinguishing between good and bad political projects or for deciding to do one thing rather than another. This, again, is an unfortunate misreading of what I said: 'everything figures, not with what stands next to it, but with the whole'. Those who are accustomed to judge everything in relation to 'justice', or 'solidarity', or 'welfare' or some other abstract 'principle', and know no other way of thinking and speaking, may perhaps be asked to consider how, in fact, a barrister in a Court of Appeal argues the inadequacy of the damages awarded to his client. Does he say, 'This is a glaring injustice', and leave it at that? Or may he be expected to say that the damages awarded are 'out of line with the general level of damages currently being awarded in libel actions'? And if he says this, or something like it, is he to be properly accused of not engaging in argument of any sort, or of having no standard or criterion, or of merely referring to 'what was done last time'? (Cf. Aristotle, *Analytica Priora*, ii 23) Again, is Mr. N. A. Swanson all at sea when he argues in this fashion about the revolutionary proposal that the bowler in cricket should be allowed to 'throw' the ball: 'the present bowling action

has evolved as a sequence, from under-arm by way of round-arm to over-arm, by successive legislation of unorthodox actions. Now, I maintain that the "throw" has no place in this sequence...'? Or, is Mr. G. H. Fender arguing without a standard or criterion, or is he merely expressing a 'hunch', when he contends that the 'throw' *has* a place in this sequence and should be permitted? And is it so far-fetched to describe what is being done here and elsewhere as 'exploring the intimations' of the total situation? And, whatever we like to say in order to bolster up our self-esteem, is not this the manner in which changes take place in the design of anything: furniture, clothes, motor cars and societies capable of political activity? Does it all become much more intelligible if we exclude circumstance and translate it into idiom of 'principles', the bowler, perhaps, arguing his 'natural right' to throw? And, even then, can we exclude circumstance: would there ever be a question of the right to throw if the right to bowl over-arm had not already been conceded? At all events, I may perhaps be allowed to reiterate my view that moral and political 'principles' are abridgements of traditional manners of behaviour, and to refer specific conduct to 'principles' is not what it is made to appear (viz. referring it to a criterion which is reliable because it is devoid of contingency, like a so-called 'just price').

4. It has been asserted that in politics there is no 'total situation': 'why should we presuppose that, inside the territory we call Britain...there is only one society, with one tradition? Why should not there be two societies...each with its own way of life?' In the understanding of a more profound critic this might be a philosophical question which would require something more than a short answer. But in the circumstances perhaps it is enough to say: first, that the absence of homogeneity does not necessarily destroy singleness; secondly, what we are considering here is a legally organized society and we are considering the manner in which its legal structure (which in spite of its incoherencies cannot be supposed to have a competitor) is reformed and amended; and thirdly, I stated (on p. 147) what I meant by a 'single community' and my reasons for making this my starting-place.

5. Lastly, it has been said that, since I reject 'general principles', I provide no means for detecting incoherencies and for determining what shall be on the agenda of reform. 'How do we discover what a society [sic] intimates?' But to this I can only reply: 'Do you want to be told that in politics there is, what certainly exists nowhere else, a mistake-proof manner of deciding what should be done?' How does a scientist, with the current con-

dition of physics before him, decide upon a direction of profitable advance? What considerations passed through the minds of medieval builders when they detected the inappropriateness of building in stones as if they were building in wood? How does a critic arrive at the judgement that a picture is incoherent, that the artist's treatment of some passages is inconsistent with his treatment of others?

Mill,[8] when he abandoned reference to general principle either as a reliable guide in political activity or as a satisfactory explanatory device, put in its place a 'theory of human progress' and what he called a 'philosophy of history'. The view I have expressed in this essay may be taken to represent a further stage in this intellectual pilgrimage, a stage reached when neither 'principle' (on account of what it turns out to be: a mere index of concrete behaviour) nor any general theory about the character and direction of social change seems to supply an adequate reference for explanation or for practical conduct.

[8] J. S. Mill, *Autobiography* (Oxford: Oxford University Press, 1971), pp. 136–7, 144–5.

INDEX

INDEX

INDEX

Shakespeare, 19, 40, 51
Skill(s), 4, 25, 26, 28, 45, 48, 50–55,
    57, 70, 74, 78, 79, 81, 82, 86, 88,
    90, 92, 150
Social design, 6, 83
Social sciences, 32, 34, 35, 89
Socialization, 31, 34, 79, 80, 82,
    84–7, 90, 91, 94
Society(ies), 5n, 12, 25, 35, 65, 79,
    81, 84, 85, 91, 92, 96, 101, 103,
    107, 108, 110, 115, 116, 123,
    126, 133, 137–49, 152, 153, 154,
    157
Society for Promoting Christian
    Knowledge, 81
Sociology, 34, 36, 37, 93
Socrates, 16
Socratic, 10
Solidarité de sottise, 91
Spanish, 56
Specialisms, 118, 123, 126, 131–3
Studies, liberal, 30
Studium, 96
Style, 56, 61, 62, 139, 140, 141, 142,
    145, 146
Summa Theologica (St. Thomas
    Aquinas), 122, 134
Swanson, N. A., 156
Switzerland, 149n
Sympathy, 12, 99, 147, 149
Symposiarch, 13, 14

Teacher(s), 6, 38, 45–50, 56–8,
    60–62, 68–70, 72, 75, 76, 80,
    94, 97, 99, 100, 101, 105, 107
Teaching, definition of, 11, 16, 44,
    46, 47, 48, 50, 56, 57, 61, 62, 70,
    78, 79, 81n, 84, 87, 92, 101, 103,
    104, 108, 122, 133
Techne, 126, 133, 134
Techne chrematistike, 133
Technical College, 82, 87
Technology, 6, 112
Tenedos, 40
Theology, Augustinian, 29
Thucydides, 148
Toulouse, 29
Tower of Babel, 5n

Transaction(s), 17n, 23, 25, 63–71,
    93, 94, 148
Two cultures, 33

*Über die Zukunft unserer Bildungs-
    anstalten* (Friedrich Nietzsche),
    31, 79n
Ulysses, 31
Undergraduate(s), 92, 97, 100, 101,
    102, 104, 107, 112, 115, 117,
    120, 121, 124, 125, 126, 128,
    129, 130, 131, 132, 133, 134
United Nations, 40
United States, 2, 3
Universities
    American, 6, 123, 125
    British, 90, 105, 106, 117, 119,
        125, 126
University
    definition of, 87, 92, 96–101, 103,
        107, 111, 121, 122, 123, 125,
        126, 127, 128, 132, 133, 134
    idea of, 3, 95, 96, 100, 103
Utility, 6, 26, 27

Valéry, Paul, 17, 37
Venice, 45
Voice(s), 38, 39, 126
'The Voice of Poetry in the
    Conversation of Mankind'
    (Michael Oakeshott), 13n
Vulcan, 25

Wabash river, 40
Watson, James, 22
Weltanschauung, 119, 121, 123, 124
Westminster College, 85, 91
Whewell, 119
White House, 106
Working Papers of the Schools
    Council, 84n

Xenophon, 46n.

Zeuxis, 154

ACKNOWLEDGEMENTS

'A Place of Learning' was first presented as the Abbott Memorial Lecture in the Social Sciences at Colorado College in September 1974. It is reproduced in *The Colorado College Studies* 12, Colorado Springs, 1975

'Learning and Teaching' was first published in *The Concept of Education*, edited by R. S. Peters (London: Routledge and Kegan Paul, 1967)

'Education: The Engagement and its Frustration' was first published in *Education and the Development of Reason*, edited by R. F. Dearden, P. H. Hearst and R. S. Peters (London: Routledge and Kegan Paul, 1972)

'The Idea of a University' was first published in *The Listener*, XLIII, 1950

'The Universities' was first published in the *Cambridge Journal*, II, 1948–9

'Political Education' was presented as an inaugural lecture at the London School of Economics and was first published in *Rationalism and Politics* (London: Methuen & Co Ltd, 1962)